Criminal Justice
Recent Scholarship

Edited by
Marilyn McShane and Frank P. Williams III

A Series from LFB Scholarly

Arrest Discretion of Police Officers
The Impact of Varying Organizational Structures

Richard F. Groeneveld

LFB Scholarly Publishing LLC
New York 2005

Library of Congress Cataloging-in-Publication Data

Groeneveld, Richard F., 1956-
  Arrest discretion of police officers : the impact of varying
organizational structures / Richard F. Groeneveld.
     p. cm. -- (Criminal justice)
  Includes bibliographical references and index.
  ISBN 1-59332-125-2 (alk. paper)
  1. Police discretion--United States. 2. Arrest (Police method)--United
States--Decision making. 3. Organizational behavior--United States. 4.
Police administration--United States. 5. Police--Research. 6.
Organization--Research. I. Title. II. Series: Criminal justice (LFB
Scholarly Publishing LLC).
  HV7936.D54G76 2005
  363.2'3--dc22

2005012790

ISBN 1-59332-125-2

Printed on acid-free 250-year-life paper.

Manufactured in the United States of America.

CONTENTS

List of Tables   vii

List of Figures   ix

Acknowledgments   xi

CHAPTER 1: **The Arrest Decision**   1

CHAPTER 2: **Police Discretion and Professional Policing**   13

CHAPTER 3: **Measuring Organizational Influence**   75

CHAPTER 4: **How Police Agencies Attempt to Influence
        Discretion**   97

CHAPTER 5: **Implications for Law Enforcement
        Practitioners**   121

Appendix: Research Questionnaire   141

References   147

Index   155

LIST OF TABLES

Tables

1. Likert Scale Categories for Survey Instrument   88

2. Comparison of Police Departments by State Between
         Respondents and Nonrespondents   98

3. Police Departments by Number of Sworn Officers (size)
         Showing Respondents and Nonrespondents   100

4. Police Departments by United States Region Showing
         Surveys Sent and Those Returned   101

5. Police Departments by United States Region Showing
         Requests for Research Summary   102

6. Arrest Discretion Control Scale (ADCS) Score Summary   104

7. Summary Statistics for Dimensional Scales   107

8. Number of Supervisory Levels Within the Organization   108

9. Number of Work Divisions Within the Police Department   109

10. Entry Level Education Within the Police Department   110

11. Number of Specialty Details Within the Police Department   111

12. Number of Sworn Officers in the Department   112

13. Supervisory Span of Control Within the Police Department   113

14. Predictor Summary Statistics and Correlations   117

15. Regression Summary Statistics   118

16. Summary Statistics for Dimensional Predictors   125

LIST OF FIGURES

Figures

1. Generalized role set in a use of force incident   31

2. Classification of police departments   54

3. Organizational styles and their influence on discretion   77

Acknowledgments

Many people have contributed to the completion of this book. First, of course, gratitude is extended to the contributors of each of the police departments across the country that responded to the survey questionnaire. They gave valuable time out of their schedules to provide the foundation for this research. I never cease to be amazed at the tenacity of law enforcement administrators to seek knowledge for the advancement of the profession. I am proud to be a member of this family.

I am particularly grateful for the patient guidance of Dr. N. Joseph Cayer. Joe's unruffled wisdom lead me to higher potential than I ever imagined could be achieved. He channeled my efforts towards a multitude of viewpoints and theoretical orientations representative of contemporary thinking. I am also thankful for the support of my colleagues Dr. Ronald Perry and Dr. John Hepburn. Ron's energy seemed endless, and aggravating at times, as he drove me to understand concepts and protocols as they relate to the methods of scientific inquiry. He forced me to look at the world through different lenses and toughest of all, to think. In addition, I want to thank John for his challenging insight and helpful encouragement, which always kept me on my toes. John taught me that research without purpose and focus is useless for the field.

Finally, I wish to thank my colleagues and superiors at the Phoenix Police Department. Without their support the completion of this work would still be a question mark.

CHAPTER 1

The Arrest Decision

There has been significant discussion by legal and academic scholars, practitioners, politicians, and the community as to the core function of law enforcement. In particular as it applies to the arrest decision process. This book examines the influence of organizational characteristics on street-level discretion (decision-making) by police officers in making field arrests.

While there has been considerable research focus placed on individual, situational, and even community level indicators regarding police discretionary behavior, little has been done in the area of organizational effects. A review of the literature strongly suggests that such organizational indicators can have a significant impact on influencing such areas as police use of force (Skolnick and Fyfe, 1993). However, the effect of organizational variables on police arrest behavior seems to be unresolved (Riksheim and Chermak, 1993).

The concept of police discretion itself is relatively new, with many scholars pointing to the American Bar Foundation (ABF) study of the mid 1950s as the premier "discovery" event that changed the ministerial paradigm of policing, to one that recognized the existence of discretionary decision-making (Davis, 1975). Up to this point, many police administrators refused to even acknowledge that discretion played a part in policing. For clarity of this research, police discretion is operationalized through a mixture of characterizations providing a contemporary definition as follows:

> Police discretion exists when officers have some leeway or choice in how to respond to a situation. The fewer the rules about handling incidents and situations, the more discretion officers can exercise. Discretion involves both action and inaction (Davis, 1968; Ericson, 1982).

1

The literature presents several assumptions that help guide the focus of this study. First, the complexity of police work has two dimensions; the complexity of the situations presented to the police, and the complexity of the police response to those situations. Second, discretion is unavoidable, the real problem is uncontrolled discretion. Third, levels of discretion are contingent on the flexibility that police departments allow their officers by policy or lack of policy. Fourth, that properly controlled, discretion has certain positive features. Fifth, organizational dimensions can be defined to measure the capacity of discretion and control within the organization. Finally, a scale or index can be developed to measure such levels of discretion at a range of low (controlled discretion) to high (unfettered discretion).

The past two decades have seen growing awareness of the complexity of police work and an examination of the use of discretion in officers' daily policing activities. While the routine nature of police work tends to obscure the complexities involved with police discretion, few would argue that such decision-making is inconsequential. In fact, the point that a police officer's duties compel him to exercise personal discretion many times throughout a day is clearly evident, sometimes with catastrophic results. In a society that places tremendous value in personal liberty, the management of discretion by police officers can become a critical and difficult exercise.

This research is intended to provide some insight and help close the gap in existing theory involving organizational structures and their impact on discretionary choices. Theories at the organizational level of analysis – systems theory, organizational theories (e.g., structure and processes), and contingency theory (decision-making) – are at the core of the empirical and conceptual components that drive this research.

Purpose

Historically, the police have asserted authority in many ways, often having nothing to do with arrest. Nonetheless, the arrest decision can have a significant and pervasive effect, not only on the arrestee, but also on the organization. Critical decision areas, such as the use of deadly force, have obvious impacts on the organization and have been heavily researched (Skolnick and Fyfe, 1993). However, the arrest decision, one that impacts the liberty of approximately 14 million people each year (FBI Uniform Crime Reports, 2003), seems to merit serious critical review. Critics claim that this decision (arrest) is largely ungoverned, and that police training goes a long way in teaching technique (i.e., approach, handcuffing, frisk, and so on), but does little to address the substantive issue of protecting citizen rights. The emphasis on mechanics and the neglect of substantive decisions are very similar to the state of police practices regarding deadly force thirty years ago. Thus, a central question for this study becomes, "In what ways do organizational structures influence the arrest decisions of patrol officers?"

Police executives' past efforts to control unnecessary discretion have had less than stellar results. Kelling (1999) argues that discretion in policing seems to be widely acknowledged, however, there does not seem to be any appreciable impact in administration despite such knowledge. In general, much of the organizational control apparatus for law enforcement agencies is mired in the earlier forms of command and control, quasi-military training, line and staff models of supervision, and rigid structures of rules and regulations. Such control mechanisms, an outgrowth of the Taylor model, have been around for most of the 20th century. In fact, some scholars argue that such controls have had tragic, unanticipated consequences for law enforcement organizations. Kelling provides another example as the bitter anti-management culture that is representative in many police departments to this day. Such a culture represents a "stay out of trouble" (de-policing) attitude that alienates officers from the community (p. 7).

In 1980, Lawrence Sherman reviewed two decades of quantitative research examining the causes of police behavior in the United States. In the early nineties, Riksheim and Chermak (1993) did a comparative analysis of Sherman's studies against research completed in the 1980s in similar areas of police behavior, which included the arrest variable. They found that whereas individual and situational characteristics were present, organizational factors were not even considered in the arrest process for the pre-1980s studies. In fact, organizational indicators received the least amount of quantitative attention during the 1980s research, despite the fact that they appeared to be consistent predictors of police behavior (p. 377). Riksheim and Chermak point out that studies examining organizational factors suggest significant variation among police agencies across the United States. In addition, explicit attempts to test theoretically derived propositions or hypotheses appeared uncommon, and theoretical explanations of quantitative findings were even less frequent in the studies.

Current theory has been inadequate in elucidating the phenomena of police discretion with respect to the organization, especially in informed explanations or propositions on how to guide such discretion. This is a significant problem since the prevailing view is that organizational factors are those over which police agencies have the most direct control. The challenge comes with reference to indoctrinating line officers as to the differences of proper discretion and "unnecessary," or improper discretion. Ironically, practitioners have used the term "common sense" to illustrate much of the discretionary behavior needed for police work; however, such a vague and ambiguous expression is inadequate for the true complexities involving such professional judgment.

In sum, the arrest decision represents a major gap when placed in the conceptual area of discretion control. There is good reason to ruminate on those factors that impact the critical arrest decision, especially in the area of the organizational level of scrutiny, which has been gravely lacking. This volume will explore such phenomena in the hopes of leading to a better understanding of such objects.

Police Administration and Discretion

Criminal justice scholars, elected officials, and police administrators have long acknowledged that the nature of police service creates serious potential problems for accountability. Because police officers routinely exercise discretion in a broad range of decisions affecting the life and liberty of citizens, it seems apparent that the justice process should require great commitment to developing organizational structures and policy guidelines that set standards, shape the inevitable use of discretion, and support community involvement.

Clearly, the police have awesome power in that they have the ability to take human life, deprive citizens of their liberty by arrest and detention, and can utilize physical force to obtain compliance. What is less clear are the methods by which the police should be, and can be, held accountable to the community they serve.

This is not to say that American society does not have mechanisms in place for accountability. On the contrary, Walker (2001) describes several primary mechanisms that are clearly noticeable to the general public. Walker displays these mechanisms as the *Political System*, the

Courts, and *Professional Police Administration.* He argues that the primary mechanism for holding the police accountable in a democracy is the political system (pg. 9). This is accomplished through elected officials who appoint police chiefs and control department budgets. It is expected that elected officials will be responsible for directing the police and seeing that they reflect the will of the people. However, many see the political system as a failure of accountability and have turned to the courts. The explosion of civil rights and civil liberties has opened the door for courts to be used to remedy what is seen as habitual and egregious misconduct of police, especially in terms of pattern and practice. But even the courts have limitations as a mechanism of accountability. Many instances of police misconduct never make it to the court system. Finally is professional police administration, which many police executives argue is the most advantageous point to impact police misconduct. Despite significant accomplishments in many areas (e.g., recruitment, training, and retention), critics maintain that such a mechanism has not necessarily been shown to be effective up to now. While this list is not all-inclusive of accountability mechanisms (civilian oversight, arbitration, consent decrees, and so on), it does illustrate some of the main dimensions. However, this study maintains its focus on the area of *Professional Police Administration.*

Concept of Police Discretion

Kenneth Culp Davis (1975), in his book *Police Discretion*, illustrated the need for administrative rulemaking in restricting the discretionary behavior of police. Nonetheless, even Davis lamented the need for significant discretion on the part of police officers in conducting such a human service activity. But Davis was concerned with the problem of accountability and the fact that officers generally work alone, mostly free from direct observation of their supervisors.

Much of the research into police misconduct has used the individual as the unit of analysis. A new focus is emerging in which the examination is directed toward the police organization (Cannon, 1997). As early as the Wickersham Commission (1931), and more recently with the Christopher Commission (1991) and Rampart Area Corruption Investigation (2000), officials have been looking at the breakdown or lack of accountability mechanisms that lead to organizational dysfunction (Davis, 1975; Kelling, 1999; Walker, 2001).

Police administrators are beginning to realize that putting officers on the streets in a timely and organized fashion and getting them to particular locations rapidly is quite different from shaping police behavior once officers are out in the community dealing with citizens' problems, needs, and conflicts. Even Davis (1975), a strong proponent of "administrative rule-making," quickly acknowledged the need for discretion at the line level if the criminal justice system was to have any hope of operating effectively. Yet, Kelling (1999) warns that such empowerment begs questions from inside and outside the organization if we are to understand the delicate balance of discretionary decision-making and accountability.

"What is the proper balance between individual rights and community interests? What do community collaboration, cooperation, and accountability really mean in an operational sense? How are police kept from protecting narrow parochial interests – such as keeping 'strangers' out of neighborhoods and communities? How do police refrain from doing what citizens should do for themselves or from usurping the roles of private or other governmental agencies?" (p. 12).

The exercise of discretion is not a simple matter. In most cases, the officer chooses one of several possible alternatives. Thus, controlling discretion is usually not a matter of simply forbidding something; it is more often a matter of encouraging officers to choose one option over another. Add to this the arrest decision, which is extremely complex and can have significantly dangerous consequences for the officer, the suspect, and the organization. Consider a study of felony arrests done by Petersilia, Abrahamse, and Wilson (1987), that found that supervisors had little interest in the "quality" of arrests measured in terms of their ultimate outcomes. This is a disturbing declaration when associated with the allegation that most arrests do not result in formal criminal prosecution, much less conviction (Walker, 1993).

Theoretical Framework

The appropriate role of police is an area where there is some dissension among scholars; although, it is generally agreed that, in practice, police have multiple functions, many of which involve situations where no crime has occurred. The community, the law, and the policing organization provide the officer with rules, and these rules provide the officer with a sense of order —what the officer perceives as appropriate conduct (Ericson, 1982). Scholars suggest that police officers act on the basis of predispositions or overall orientations and these predispositions provide an interpretive framework in which the situational cues are evaluated (Wilson, 1968; Smith and Klein, 1983; Brown, 1988). Predispositions supply the officer with a repertoire of possible behavior and, from this collection, the officer selects an appropriate response to a specific situation. While there exists intuitive support for the connection between police discretion and organizational predispositions, little empirical research has been conducted to examine this issue.

For purposes of this research, it is necessary to identify the conceptual context of organizations being studied. Using Wilson's (1968) pioneering work of cross-classification of police agencies, police departments can be categorized under one of four groupings. These classifications revolve around the concepts of bureaucratization and professionalism (Smith and Klein, 1983). Wilson divides professional police agencies into service and legalistic styles, depending on their degree of bureaucratization. All nonprofessional departments are considered to operate under a watchman style, independent of their level of bureaucratization. Nonprofessional police agencies with shallow bureaucracies are labeled *fraternal,* while nonprofessional, bureaucratic police agencies are labeled *militaristic.* *Service* and *legalistic* departments are professional agencies that vary in terms of bureaucratization.

Wilson argues that it is possible to determine whether top administrators in different types of police agencies hold different conceptions of the police role and have different expectations regarding appropriate police behavior. Smith and Klein (1983) found that such organizational properties did influence the probability of arrest, and more importantly, that certain situational variables on the decision to arrest were conditional on the organizational context in which the encounter occurred (p. 92). Thus, on one dimension there appears to be support for the thesis that differences in organizational ethos covary with structural characteristics of police agencies (i.e., bureaucratization and professionalism).

These suppositions are based on the premise that the exercise of discretion can be developed into an operational style preconditioned by the organization. Brown (1988) supports this by pointing out that discretion is value based and those values can be preconditioned by the organization (i.e., service, order maintenance, crime control), and such preconditions affect the arrest decision.

The classifications elaborated by Wilson, and used by Smith and Klein, have been applied in this study toward the design of a scale to establish ordinal categories for the variables being measured. Such a scale presents a continuum that displays where agencies might fall along the classifications described by Wilson.

Organizational Correlates of Police Discretion

The exercise of police discretion can be a difficult notion to quantify; however, conceptualizing those dimensions that impact our dependent variable (organizational influence of police discretion in field arrests) helps to provide a level of precision for measurement. Since the unit of observation is the organization, this study will focus on the structural characteristics of bureaucracies.

Review of the literature provides significant groundwork in identifying *inter-* and *intra*-organizational indicators that relate to police behavior. In order to establish validity to this research it is necessary to distinguish those organizational correlates that have been suggested as having a significant impact on organizational influence (dependent variable) at the arrest decision point. The independent variables identified for this research deal with characteristics of the police department and are internal to the organization. For purposes of this inquiry they include the following: 1) how bureaucratic the police agency is, 2) the level of professionalism of the department, 3) the size of the police department, and 4) supervision levels (span of control). Each of these variables is explained in more detail below.

Bureaucracy
The word "bureaucracy" has been used rather loosely in the police literature, but there does appear to be some consensus on the characteristics that bureaucratic police departments share. Bureaucratic police departments are thought to have a high degree of vertical differentiation (a tall rank structure), in which efficiency, discipline, and productivity are stressed (Bittner, 1970; Manning, 1997). This

high degree towards the military model tends to stress regulations, hierarchy, and obedience (Skolnick, 1966). Officers learn to place high importance on following the rules to avoid punishment, and this rigid conception of order places emphasis on crime control behavior. For purposes of this study, bureaucracy is operationalized as the number of levels of management between the police chief and line-level officers, and the number of divisions within the department.

Professionalism

Professional police organizations have been characterized in many different ways, but are thought to be agencies in which education, service, and citizen respect are central (Goldstein, 1977). Professional departments may have tall or shallow rank structure but generally have wide ranges of specialty units. Having specialty units (e.g., crime prevention unit, community relations, school resource officer, etc.) is believed to demonstrate a department's commitment to community service. In addition, professional police departments may be identified by various factors such as college incentive pay, community relations training, and percentage of officers who are college educated (Smith and Klein, 1983). It is postulated that the more professional (service-oriented) a department is the more inclined its focus is towards quality of life issues than with prosecutions.

For purposes of this study, a mix of Crank's (1990) and Goldstein's (1977) characterization of professionalism will be operationalized as follows; 1) the amount of entry level education required for police officers, and 2) the number of specialty units within the organization.

Department Size

While department size can be measured in a variety of ways, this study will focus on the number of sworn personnel in a department. Research is mixed on the impact of department size on discretionary decisions to arrest. Mastrofski, Ritti, and Hoffmaster (1987) found that officers in smaller departments were more likely to arrest than their larger department counterparts. The willingness of officers to arrest decreased as department size and level of bureaucracy increased. However, Brown (1988) found that officers in large departments experienced more latitude and autonomy and were more inclined to act (arrest). There is the presumption that large departments have less effective controls on their members, less group stability, and a weaker link to the community that tends to subtract from the service style of policing. This makes it difficult to describe whether the relationship of size will have a direct or inverse relationship with discretionary influence. However, it is believed that measures of size will be inversely correlated with department influence of arrest discretion.

Supervision

This deals with the span of control for field (street) supervisors. One obvious way a supervisor has of influencing discretion and maintaining some control over patrol officers is simply by being present at the scene of a call. Those police departments that have a high number of officers for each supervisor are expected to have less effective controls on their members. Interestingly, some research found that the presence of police supervisors increased the likelihood of arrest. Smith and Klein (1983) found that militaristic and legalistic departments, especially, produced more arrests when an on-scene supervisor was present. Kelling argues that in today's litigious society, along with the risk of discipline involved in improper arrest procedures, that officers are more likely to avoid arrest situations if at all possible. Lack of supervision can enhance such avoidance.

For purposes of this study, supervision will be operationalized as the number of patrol officers normally assigned to one field supervisor, keeping in mind that many agencies have policy limits on span of control even though the actual numbers may fluctuate slightly. It is presumed that the lower the ratio of employees to field supervisors the higher the level of control over discretionary decision making.

The importance in studying these correlates is based on the belief that the execution of public policy, as it applies to field arrests, is determined more on the basis of internally generated bureaucratic pressures, than on the nature of clientele or the demands of interest groups.

Research Questions

Several research questions have been developed to focus attention on the relationships among variables that have theoretical importance for this study. Based on review of the literature and certain expectations involving the listed variables, the following questions describe the possible links between the correlates presented and the organizational influence on police officer discretion in field arrests. The first research question is concerned with the observation of central tendency and dispersion of police departments studied along a scaled range of organizational influence over arrest discretion. The remaining research questions are descriptive in their effort to examine organizational influence over arrest discretion. The research questions are as follows:

1. What is the observed range of organizational influence on police officer discretion in field arrests among police departments as measured on a summated scale (ADCS)?

2. What is the relationship between bureaucracy and the organizational influence on police discretion in field arrests?

3. What is the relationship between professionalism and the organizational influence on police discretion in field arrests?

4. What is the relationship between department size and the organizational influence on police discretion in field arrests?

5. What is the relationship between supervisory span of control and the organizational influence on police discretion in field arrests?

Delimitations and Limitations of the Study

Certain factors that may affect this research come under the control of the researcher, others do not. A significant delimitation involves the size and nature of the group being questioned. For practicality, the sample for this study is restricted to municipal law enforcement agencies with 200 or more sworn officers located within the United States. This raises the issue of validity as to whether research results will apply to smaller agencies, non-municipal agencies, and those that reside outside the United States. Review of the literature indicates that smaller police departments have lesser-delineated structures of bureaucracy and professionalism indicating the potential for higher levels of officer discretion that would not be captured in the study. While similar results may be found in police agencies in developed countries, it is unclear how such results would apply in undeveloped countries.

By using a survey questionnaire, a common limitation is the willingness of individuals to respond at all, to respond in a timely fashion, and to respond accurately. This has important possible effects on the outcomes of the study that are not controllable by the researcher.

Another limitation that needs to be clearly specified is that of the identified variables for this study. While research in the area of police discretion is limited, and has only recently come to the forefront, there is much to be learned about the cause and effect factors. There are but four factors being measured in their applicability to the problem at hand in this research. This creates questions as to the pertinence of such organizational variables and the missing elements that may play a more vital role in police discretion. In addition, the theoretical component involving police discretion at the organizational level is associated with a variety of frameworks that fails to provide a single construct for analysis. The operationalization of police discretion in this study may not correlate well to future research. However, it is believed that such examination is instrumental in establishing foci for future research and will help to lay the groundwork for such studies.

CHAPTER 2

Police Discretion and Professional Policing

This chapter provides an overview to relevant literature in the field of law enforcement and public administration in this country. The purpose is to identify the eminent scholars in the field of police administration, the parameters of police discretion, and which ideas, theories, questions, and hypotheses seem most important in the arrest decision process for police as they relate to the organizational unit of analysis.

This review focuses on the early years of police administration in the United States and organizes discussion around key variables and concepts that apply to social control and police discretion. In addition, the review explores early and contemporary research, theoretical frameworks, influences on governance and policymaking, and the impact of community policing in the arrest decision process.

The study of police discretion itself is a relatively new phenomenon. Therefore, the literature review does not lend itself to a linear, chronological order. The format for this study may be visualized as overlapping planes, or dimensions, encompassed by the general topic of police administration in the United States. Each of these planes illustrates narrow sections of topic areas such as professional policing, organization theory, the concept of police discretion, and accountability. In each subsequent section the literature review moves closer to the specific theoretical frameworks and organizational characteristics that impact police discretion, especially as they relate to field arrests.

The literature reveals that at no other time in American History, including the tumultuous and violent era of the civil-rights movement, has law enforcement come under such intense scrutiny from so manysegments of our society. The community effort to control police behavior in the areas of use of force, civil rights violations, police policy and procedure, and corruption are having significant impacts on police organizations. Whether good or bad, effective or not, such controls continue to be argued by critics and proponents of the police. One area that seems to generate universal agreement is the difficulty for police executives and public administrators to control unwanted behavior by officers. The complexities of the organizational structure, shift in societal norms, strong presence of union stewardship, and emphasis on individual rights has made the control of deviant and illegal practices by police officers a most perplexing challenge.

This literature review raises some fundamental issues for police administrators. A significant number of social science studies of the police have focused on the analysis and consequences of individual officer behavior and not on collective actions by police officers to influence law enforcement policy. As larger municipal agencies move toward a joint management-labor determination of goals and administration under the prodding of activist employee associations, the absence of in-depth studies of police from a group perspective becomes more significant (Horton, 1970; Kaufman, 1969).

Another fundamental issue for police executives involves that of accountability. If policing is truly a professional commitment, then it is only fitting that executives and administrators give high priority to accountability. Arguably, certain characteristics of community policing threaten police officer accountability. Such characteristics as decentralization, greater discretion at the street level, closer citizen interaction, and development of problem-solving and street tactics by patrol officers will require a delicate balance of empowerment and answerability. This review is presented to help narrow the focus of the research problem and to reinforce the need for the proposed research study.

Professional Policing in the United States

Society has utilized formal mechanisms to enforce social control since ancient times. Yet, public administration and police policy are fairly new processes in this country. In fact, most tenets of the professional policing model seen in the United States today come from 18th century England, and somewhat later, through the vision of Sir Robert Peel. While some historians question the credit given Peel for professional policing, he had managed by 1829 to establish a full-time day and night patrol force in London (Reynolds, 1998). Interestingly, the public had a rather ambivalent attitude about the police in general, especially their use of force. In fact, had it not been for the greater fear that the public had of riots and crime that was occurring in the early nineteenth century, their fear about the abuses of power by an organized police agency might have extinguished such an institution (Skolnick & Fyfe, 1993). Peel was sympathetic to this public sentiment, and even though his organizational chart imitated the military structure, he wanted the police distinguishable from the army. The most significant sign was the issuance of blue coats for the police instead of the traditional military "red coats."

However, policing in the United States has been painstakingly slow in its growth and development. The historical and social perspectives of police administration are essential to know if one is to have a basic understanding of the differing viewpoints of those persons who have been, and currently are, police leaders. In addition, consideration needs to be given to the role of the public administrator and the police. For most local, county, state and federal bureaucracies, law enforcement is one of the most costly and politically visible aspects of administration (Goldstein, 1990; Pate & Fridell, 1993; Skolnick & Fyfe, 1993; Cannon, 1997).

A review of the literature demonstrates that policymaking for the police has traditionally been left to police administrators and the courts (Skolnick & McCoy, 1984). This raises several questions. How involved should public administrators, politicians, and the community be in policy decisions regarding their law enforcement agencies? How often do ideas come from people like policy analysts, researchers, academics, and consultants? How important are the mass media in focusing officials' attention on some of these problems and contributing to their neglect in others?

Kingdon (1984) argues that a significant influence on policy-making agendas is a crisis or prominent event that represents a crucial problem. Unfortunately, this seems to be the customary catalyst for law enforcement to react. If the problem, policy, and politics of such a crisis, something Kingdon refers to as "streams," can come together at certain times then the opportunity for a policy window may present itself (p. 21). The question then begs itself, are public administrators and law enforcement executives looking at such windows as opportunity or impediment?

Because of the diversity of our community members it becomes difficult, if not impossible, for an administrator to develop police policy that will not be subject to criticism. Many perceptions from the public about what police should be doing add to the confusion and misunderstanding of the police role in the community. In fact, Pogrebin and Regoli (1986) argue that police organizations are often the most criticized of public agencies in the government sector. The problem is compounded by typically heterogeneous communities that insist on varying priorities for and needs from the police.

Goldstein (1990) explains that it has only been during the past three decades that policing has received serious scholarly attention. Such attention has led to increased openness and review of police work, along with research and experimentation. Goldstein points out that much of police history in the United States has been devoid of any critical thinking up until the 1950s. Police departments and administrators have seemed to be one step behind a rapidly changing society. It was not until the gap became so great, or a scandal surfaced, that the push to *reform* arose. In fact, the term "reform" itself seems to be the buzzword for giving the appearance that administrators are dealing with police failures. But are administrators taking full advantage of these policy windows that Kingdon describes?

J. Q. Wilson (1968) points out that policymaking for police tends to be further convoluted by the fact that law enforcement organizations, especially the larger ones, maintain objectives that either cannot be obtained or are in direct conflict of operations. For example, many social scientists agree that the police have a small amount of control over the level of crime in their community; however, almost all agencies are heavily evaluated on their efforts in reducing crime from year to year. When the crime rates go up, as they will surely do at some point, the programs and policies of the police tend to come under scrutiny and criticism. This can be further aggravated by proactive police efforts directed towards citizens to report criminal activity thereby, raising crime rates. Then there is the apprehension of criminals. While this is an important part of police work covered extensively by policy and procedure, it is a relatively small portion of an officer's activity. Conversely, police officers spend the majority of their time in social conflict resolution situations without a well-defined notion of what their actual roles are in such non-law enforcement activities.

If we agree with Wilson's point regarding faulty policymaking, then police executives and public administrators must understand the importance of first establishing indicators on what constitutes satisfactory performance for the organization and the community, and the strategies on how to pursue such performance. The issues and challenges of policy development for police raised in this section have evolved incrementally over time. To better understand how such issues have come to the forefront requires a review of the roots of American policing.

Early Years of Police Administration

The roots of professional policing in this country that stemmed from England's Peelian Reform of 1829 quickly took on uniquely American characteristics in the United States. From the mid to late 1800s, policing in America became the most decentralized in the world, spreading across 16,000 jurisdictions (Pate & Fridell, 1993). With the exception of a few federal agencies, most American police reported to municipal, county, and state governments. This explains the large number of structures, policies, and procedures that differ from one locality to another. Instead of having one method or policy defining a formal mechanism for social control, there are now thousands.

A major difference between American and English policing involved the violent revolution and bloody civil war of this young American country. Violence seemed ingrained into the American culture, add to that the patented revolver (Samuel Colt) in 1835, and violence took the form of armed attacks. While the carrying of a weapon by an English "bobby" would be a severe breach of policy worthy of termination, American peace officers took it upon themselves to be *armed*, often without the permission of their supervisors.

As the ambivalence about armed police had presented itself in England in the 1700s, so had the revulsion raised its head in a young America. Many of the early peace officers in this country were considered no better than the outlaws or thugs they were being paid to defend against. However, some theorists point out that the lack of clear guidance in the form of training and policies provided to police officers was a contributing factor in the poor opinions of law enforcement (Skolnick & Fyfe 1993). These poorly trained, and sometimes-questionable peace officers, were often left to make their own decisions concerning what force to use and when to use it. Ironically, the use of force by government agents in making arrests was just as problematic then as it is today. Many of these decisions were heavily impacted by the attitudes of peers and supervisors.

Much of the image of professional policing in the United States can be traced to August Vollmer (Carte, 1975). Vollmer reigned as police chief of Berkeley, California, from 1905 to 1932. His most significant accomplishments involve the reform of policing through technology and higher personnel standards. Vollmer initiated a patrol-wide police signal system, the first completely mobile patrol --- first on bicycles, then in squad cars --- modern records systems, beat analysis, and modus operandi. The first scientific crime laboratory in the United States was set up in Berkeley in 1916, under the direction of a full time forensic scientist. The first lie detector machine to be used in criminal investigation was built in the Berkeley department in 1921. In what could be considered the first principle to community policing, Vollmer stressed crime prevention over apprehension. While the Progressives were coming and going in many cities, Vollmer was working hard and with great success to professionalize Berkeley.

As policing moved into the 20th century public attention focused on the use of force by law enforcement, often looking at those instances when it was used, or alleged to have been used, unnecessarily or to excess (Wickersham Commission, 1931). Organizational theorist O. W. Wilson (Wilson and McLaren, 1972) worried about what he referred to as "lawlessness in law enforcement," and inquired as to how to assure police accountability for its citizens. Wilson warned that public apathy toward law enforcement should not be considered approval in the satisfaction of the organization, but that slight provocation alone could tip the scales to abhorrence. Yet, Wilson opposed the creation of civilian review boards and believed largely in self-regulation of police organizations, which he felt came under the label of profession similar to doctors, dentists, and lawyers.

Wilson argued that the professional ethos would incorporate a need for the appearance, as well as the substance of justice especially in highly publicized, inflammatory cases. Increased community assistance to the police would more than offset an additional loss of personnel control, and when police actions were explained citizens might generally support the department and help protect it from unwarranted complaints. While public administration scholars developed tenets of organizational theory during the 1920s and 1930s, Wilson strongly urged their application to the police segment of government.

As policing moved into the last half of the 20th century, courts, legislatures, and law enforcement officials themselves began to provide clearer guidance concerning such areas as the use of force and arrest by police. In particular, the United States Supreme Court made several far reaching decisions concerning the legal constraints involved in the police arrest – decision process and the use of physical force upon citizens (See e.g.: *Miranda v. Arizona,* 1966; *Terry v. Ohio,* 1968; *Tennessee v. Garner,* 1985; and *Graham v. Conner,* 1989). In addition, the courts and Congress have generally imposed responsibility upon municipalities for the torts of their police officers, causing those financially stretched governments to pay more attention than ever to abuses by police officers (See *Monroe v. Pape,* 1961; and Title 42 U.S.C. Section 1983). State legislatures have enacted laws delimiting the appropriate use of force by police officers. Furthermore, law enforcement agencies have instituted more restrictive policies and procedures to limit the use of discretion by their personnel (Skolnick & Fyfe, 1993).

Use of force by the police, especially in making arrests, is a distinct function of the police and is what illustrates the difference between law enforcement and other organizations. Individual freedoms, the needs of the community, and the desire for social control are the issues that drive the discussion of the next two sections.

Democracy and Disorder

Historically the police have been looked upon as serving status quo interests. A central issue for police executives and public administrators in modern policing will be the role they play in shaping and developing social change, given its pervasiveness and accelerating rate (Reiss, 1985). Looking at civil disorder in the history of this young country, one can view the metamorphosis of the police function and how policy development has been applied, for better or worse.

Beginning in the civil war era, our nation experienced one of the most deadly riots on American shores known as the "anti-draft riots," which rocked New York City shortly after the Battle of Gettysburg in 1863. While the estimates vary, most historians agree that about 100 soldiers and civilians, many of whom were African Americans who were targeted as the reason Lincoln was fighting the war in the first place, were killed. Federal soldiers had to be diverted from around Washington D.C. to quell the outrage.

The rise of organized labor near the turn of the century meant that organized police forces were even more important than ever. Several state police forces had their beginnings and endings related to the use of police as strike breakers in factories and on railroad holdings. This had the adverse effect of developing resentment by legislatures in various parts of the country towards police who had been used to enforce the power of management over unions.

During World War II, young Hispanic men whose attire was unique, fought with soldiers and sailors home on leave during the so-called "zoot suit" riots in Los Angeles, California. Servicemen who were dating the Hispanic women of Los Angeles were involved in numerous brawls with Hispanic men over the rights to courtship. The police were often accused of enforcement that was prejudicial to the Hispanic men.

The 1960s brought the "Civil Rights Movement" into American consciousness, and was anything but boring for law enforcement. Protest marches, sit-ins, and demonstrations, particularly in the South, brought National Guard troops out as well as police dogs and horses to attack passive, mostly Black Americans expressing their constitutional rights. As free speech was taken to another level at Berkeley in 1964, America watched as students crusaded while yelling four letter words.

Television and the media were beginning to play a role in the American psyche of social unrest. Images of the Harlem riot of 1964 were brought to us by virtue of television. The images of New York cops ducking and dodging the rocks and heavy masonry being dropped on them from skyscrapers and firing their side-arms at the roofs on occasion were brought into American living rooms. Less than a year later, in August 1965, two brothers would fight with California Highway Patrol during an arrest, and the Los Angeles Police Department would get the blame for starting the Watts Riot. Innumerable buildings shooting flames into the night sky and looters carrying televisions and appliances away from shattered businesses would be occurrences that the American public would see again and again.

Riots seemed to engulf the nation in 1967 and 1968, especially in the wake of the assassination of Dr. Martin Luther King. By the late

1960s through the early 1970s, countless protests over the Vietnam War dragged on and inflamed groups large and small. Then on May 4ᵗʰ, 1970, four university students would be slain by a volley of fire from the Ohio National Guard. The effect of Kent State was considered by many media analysts as one of the most unnecessary and yet most momentous events leading up to the popular disavowal of the war in public opinion polls (Kelner and Munves, 1980).

While the National Guard was not prepared to adequately handle rowdy students, it was evident that correctional authorities in Attica, New York were not up to the task of calming the riot that took place in September of 1971. Eventually, prison authorities and state troopers stormed the prison, which resulted in inmates (guilty or not) and guards taken hostage being killed.

Such inadequacies in the face of the disorders in the 1960s, along with the massacre by the National Guard at Kent State, and the bloody fiasco at Attica in 1971, led to intervention by government officials in cities, state capitals, and Washington D.C. The hope was to teach police administrators how to better deal with riots and disorder, along with limiting human casualties. As money from Washington was forthcoming to provide training and equipment, the Vietnam War was winding down along with the rallying cry for many students in universities.

By the mid 1970s the National Task Force on Disorders and Terrorism (1976) had reported on the innumerable failures in leadership at the political and law enforcement levels. Dozens of recommendations were laid out that to this day provide a benchmark for agencies to measure their levels of readiness in the specific areas of prevention, intelligence gathering, training, inspection, and planning.

Protests did not go away in the United States, and still had the potential for damage and human suffering. Iran had tossed out the Shaw and put Ruhollah Khomeini in his place. In Beverly Hills, California, of all the unlikely places to have not one but two riots, the pro-Shaw Iranians and "patriots" of non-Iranian extraction fought the anti-Shaw Iranians on the streets and in the hills of that posh city. The Jewish Defense League and others got into the fight and the Los Angeles County Sheriff's Department and the local police department were in the middle of the fray which had its origins almost 12,000 miles away.

During the early 1980s, on the other side of the country, the City of Miami was experiencing several riots related to the police department's confrontations with members of the African American community. Both the city and the county law enforcement agencies were caught unprepared despite the recent 1976 National Task Force recommendations. Miami would move on to be among the best prepared law enforcement agencies in the nation regarding civil disorder, but the learning and readiness came at the expense of some hard lessons (Porter, 1984).

As the 1980s moved along, civil disorder seemed to disappear in this country as Americans watched uprisings in such far away places as China, Poland, Bulgaria, and East Germany. But in 1991, those countries turned their attention to Los Angeles as an amateur cameraman's tape of the Rodney King arrest involving the Los Angeles Police Department seemed like a surreal incident occurring in a foreign country. The emotions surrounding the thousands of repeat showings of that beating incubated for more than a year before the all-white jury in Simi-Valley found all four officers on trial "not guilty." As a result came the explosion of fire, gunshots, sirens and looting that set all the riot records but one for the United States history books. Only the number of people killed, some 56, did not reach the level of the previously mentioned anti-draft riots in New York (Cannon, 1997). Eventually, with police, deputies, the National Guard and even some regular army and marine units on hand, the rioters were moved off the streets. Once more, the blame was placed on a lack of adequate planning, training, and leadership by a police department that was thought to be one of the best in the world.

Of course, not all riots can be prevented, but it is the responsibility of police administrators to be ready for all sorts of unusual occurrences, such as, tornadoes, earthquakes, major fires, floods, airline crashes, hazardous materials incidents, and riots. Mayors and city managers are certainly right in expecting their law enforcement agencies to be able to cope professionally with these kinds of disasters.

The role of a police chief is one of the most demanding, challenging, and important executive functions anywhere in public administration (Vollmer, 1968; Kelly, 1975; Goldstein, 1977; and Bopp, 1984). Yet, it is imperative that these executives seek to understand the underlying causes of civil disturbance and focus their organization and policies to not be the spark that starts a disturbance.

The Dilemmas of Social Control

Wilson (1968) characterizes organizations that fail to perform to the level of expectations of society as suffering administrative problems as well as frustration. Many critics of the police have complaints that are well founded but fail to understand the conditions that lead to such failures. Wilson goes on to give examples such as, hiring unqualified police personnel, suppressing or manipulating crime reports, condoning the use of improper or illegal procedures, using patrol techniques that create tensions and irritation among citizens, and either overreacting (using too much force too quickly) or under-reacting (ignoring dangerous situations until it is too late) in the face of incipient disorder.

These criticisms are true to some extent, though the magnitude seems arguably to be exaggerated or not fully understood. Take for example the 1999 Washington, D.C. riots in which the police were accused by numerous media outlets and protest organizers of using too much force too quickly to quell the actions of WTO rioters. This came on the heels of the Seattle riots that same year that found the police substantially undermanned and under-prepared for the mass of protesters that ultimately caused six million dollars in damage to the city. Once more, when the police were slow to respond to the crowd reactions of the Los Angeles Lakers NBA championship in 2000, critics quickly pointed out the cost in damage to property and public safety perception because of a lack of action and poor organizational leadership.

Of course, without conflict and those individuals that break the law, there would be no need for police and social control. Hubert Williams (Pate & Fridell, 1993) has said that "In the best of all worlds, there would be no need for police. In that world, there would be no police and people would obey the law" (p. 5). Yet, throughout history mankind has developed formal mechanisms in society to maintain order and compliance to the law. It is only recently that police have been designated as the *formal mechanism* to provide that order maintenance.

Many social scientists maintain that the legitimate use of force by the police and their ability to detain individuals are defining characteristics of such organizations (See McLaughlin, 1992; Skolnick & Fyfe, 1993; and Pate & Fridell, 1993). If voluntary compliance were all that was required in a society, then again, the police would not be needed, or would have tremendously different missions and objectives. However, if force is a distinct function of the police, it raises a fundamental problem in a pluralist democracy. How do such organizations possess autonomy, and at the same time remain subject to control? As much as independent organizations are needed in a democracy, their independence has the potential to perpetuate injustice. Dahl (1982) explains that such independence can lead to egoism of the organization over the greater public good, and that it can even weaken or destroy democracy itself. This appears to be no more evident than in the realm of social control and the police. Even the Romans pondered the dilemma of accountability in the rule of law, as pointed out by Hubert Williams of the Police Foundation, when they asked, "*Sed quis custodiet ipsos custodies?*", or "*Who will guard the guards themselves*" (Pate and Fridell, 1993).

Social control is not new to mankind, and in America the problem is as old as our system of local government. Ever since the creation of the first precinct "houses" on this continent, the police problem has continued to grow in complexity as the years pass. As our society grows in diversity and integration, Smith (1960) argues that the flaws of police management of the organization become more visible and open to scrutiny by an ever-demanding public. Increasingly, police executives and administrators are being asked to explain why orders, policies, and procedures were developed that resulted in people being killed or seriously injured as the result of a police action. How were such policies developed that lead to tragic consequences, and what types of review were available to avoid such pitfalls?

Critics of law enforcement policy will point to recent crises such as Ruby Ridge, Waco, Rodney King, and the LAPD Rampart investigation as incidents that illustrate some of the more infamous organizational and policy failures when it comes to the topic of social control. And if these are the more prominent, only because they were captured by the American media, then how deep is the problem rooted? It becomes even more alarming in the face of at least 14 federal investigations of police departments in 13 cities being conducted by the U.S. Department of Justice in 2000. Such investigations look for patterns and practices of police misconduct, and have led to consent decrees where the Justice Department outlines certain management practices and methods in order for the city to avoid civil rights litigation. Proponents claim such tactics are necessary to guard against renegade organizations that refuse to address police misconduct, such as the Pittsburgh Police Department, which signed a decree in 1997.

The opposition claims, among other issues, that it is the federal government's way to nationalize police and take away states rights.

The powers of arrest and use of force by law enforcement officers is by no means a recent concern. This matter was reflected in the articles of the Magna Carta, imposed by the English barons on King John in 1215, reflecting a desire to prevent police abuse of power, false arrest, oppression, and contempt of the law. The compact is replete with restrictions upon the police of those days, the sheriffs, bailiffs, and constables. Interestingly, the remedies of that ancient time were similar in many ways to those proposed today: recruit better police officers, stiffen the penalties for malfeasance, and create a civilian review board as an external control upon police.

Organization Theory

Classic organization theorists saw organizations as a social device for efficiently accomplishing some stated purpose (Katz & Kahn, 1992). The focus of their attention was directed at the structures, both physical and organizational, within the unit. Little or no attention was paid to the interaction between the organization and its environment. At the same time, the human relations school of organization theory was losing favor as theorists searched for a more complete concept that helped to explain organizations.

Systems theory began to emerge as a tool for understanding human organizations following World War II. Scott (1996) noted that, "The only meaningful way to study an organization is to study it as a system." The idea behind systems thinking was the ability to contemplate the whole of a phenomenon instead of any individual part of the pattern.

This same logic, when applied to police policy, exposes the hazards of attempting the policymaking process in a vacuum. For this reason it is essential for the administrator to understand the basis of systems theory. In examining various determinants of law enforcement policies in the United States, one has to look at the organization and how it is impacted as a system; a system being that grouping of separate but interrelated components working together toward the achievement of some common objective. The police administrator of today has to be responsive to the environment (internal and external) the system is operating under.

There are numerous types and forms of organization theories such as; systems theory, public choice theory, contingency theory, theories of group politics and influence, theories of political economy, and so on. As mentioned, the traditional organization theory originally viewed law enforcement organizations as closed systems. The closed system view of the organization assumes complete rationality, optimizing performances, predictability, internal efficiency, and certainty (Robbins, 1976). Since all behavior is believed to be functional and all outcomes predictable and certain, the closed organization can ignore changes in the larger environment, such as political, technological, and economic. Thus, the closed system organization sees little need for interaction with its environment. Traditional organization theory and the closed system fall into the same stream of thinking and are compatible.

Open systems theory, on the other hand, is important to the police administrator because it tends to view the police organization with a more consistent reality; the police department is not a closed system but, rather, an open one having many dynamic interactions with the larger society in which it is embedded. Stressing the inter-relatedness of the various subsystems and the inter-relatedness of the police department with the larger world, open systems theory has the potential to foster increased cooperation. The emphasis of open systems theory upon achieving objectives serves to reinforce the need for purposeful behavior and may lead to greater effectiveness in achieving goals.

Many scholars have contributed to the foundations of general systems theory, which has its roots in biology and extends back to the 1920s and 1930s. Ludwig von Bertalanffy (1968) is generally viewed as the founding father, but the social sciences did not become fully involved until the mid- to late 1950s. It was not until the early 1970s that the theory made its way into the study of criminal justice.

Systems theories have been used to explain many aspects of an organization. The technology for resource transformation, from inputs to outputs, and the influences of various environmental conditions are often described as particular patterns of activity called systems. Systems theories point out how activities in the system are interrelated, sometimes in mathematical terms. Here events are explained as the product of natural, often unintended, patterns of interactivity. Organizational communication and control theories make frequent use of systems theory.

Law enforcement administrators have tended to view the police organization in the same way that traditional organization theorists have looked at the human organization, and that is as a "closed-system." Katz and Kahn (1992) argue that such perspectives become "arbitrary" and the reality of policy making becomes lost through their establishment. Looking at police organizations as closed-systems may help to identify boundaries, but it does not give a very accurate view of the organization. However, Munro (1979) warns that while the open-systems approach is a much more accurate view of the organization, it frequently leaves researchers in the position of having to "know everything about everything," which is a difficult posture for most empirically based scientists to obtain (p. 3).

According to Munro another challenge presents itself to police policy making. It involves what he refers to as the structural-legal versus the behavioral determinants of policy (p. 6). Constitutional bases, statutory provisions, and agency based rules and regulations are the basis on which law enforcement policy is made. This structural-legal approach, although long since abandoned by the mainstream of political science, is still the dominant strategy employed in law enforcement policy analysis.

Political scientists have known for years that behavioral determinants may be equally important, and in some instances, more important in the creation and execution of policy than the legal provisions. Munro raises the research dilemma of how an effective methodological link can be made between these two approaches so that the structural and legal policy determinants are viewed within a behavioral context. Such a link needs to be in a behavioral context in such a fashion as to be responsive to research.

To understand the concept of the open-system, Katz and Kahn (1992) discuss common characteristics of such systems in their book *The Social Psychology of Organizations (1966)*. While various types of open systems will differ, the following nine characteristics seem to define all open systems.[1]

Open systems are characterized first by the *importation of energy*. In a social organization, the energy may be in the form of people, whole institutions, material, or, most frequently, money. Once the

---

[1] For a complete summary see "The Social Psychology of Organizations," by D. Katz and R. L. Kahn, pp. 14-29. 1966 John Wiley & Sons, Inc.

energy is available to the system, it must be transformed into something usable or valuable. The transformation process is called the *throughput*. Rather obviously following the importation of energy and the throughput is the *output*, which may be material in nature or may be policies, plans, laws, or services. The nature of the output is a reflection of the purpose and operations of the organization.

The fourth characteristic of open systems is that they are *cycles of events*. This is a most important concept for the analysis of policy since it aids in the definition of institutional structures. Structures, from a social systems point of view, are defined by events that are energy exchanges, not by physical entities.

Katz and Kahn use the second law of thermodynamics to illustrate that systems move toward equilibrium. They refer to this as the entropic process, which operates in all forms of organizations to move them toward disorganization (p.251). However, open systems are characterized by *negative entropy*. The open system imports more energy than it expends. The energy is then stored in a variety of ways. Examples may include undistributed funds in bank accounts and stock in inventory may constitute negative entropy for the organization. Munro (1979) cites "organizational fat" as one such storage mode. Since open systems acquire negative entropy, they have an indefinite length of existence, depending only on their continued ability to maintain their energy requirements.

Energy alone is not sufficient for the proper functioning of an open system. The other crucial factor is information. The sixth characteristic of an open system is *information input, negative feedback*, and the *coding process*. If an organization is going to maintain itself, it must have information from its environment. This information comes generally in the form of negative feedback. A screening process, called coding, determines which inputs will actually penetrate the organization. The *coding* process then becomes crucial to the organization. It is one of the ironies of contemporary organizations that in many instances people in charge of the coding process (which really means that they control the information system) may well have little direct knowledge of the system's purposes, functions, or policies. From a policy analysis point of view, an understanding of the coding system is essential so that the analyst can appreciate the nature and adequacy of the information base being used in the analysis. The coding process also allows the organization to ingest information in a manner that allows it to make sense of an otherwise disorderly environment.

Steady state and *dynamic homeostasis* constitutes the seventh characteristic of the open system. Katz and Kahn (1992) use a biological example to illustrate the meaning of steady state with respect to open systems. They note that "the catabolic and anabolic processes of tissue breakdown and restoration within the body preserve a steady state so that the organism from time to time is not the identical organism it was but a highly similar organism" (p. 254). The steady state and dynamic homeostasis does not mean equilibrium in the usual sense of the term; rather it means that the system is maintained through dynamic processes in a recognizable form over time. "The basic principle is the preservation of the character of the system" (p. 254). In general social science terms, this could be viewed as an institutionalized change, which though constant, does not destroy the identity of the system.

Typical growth and maturation patterns of organizations and institutions is described by the open systems characteristic called *differentiation*, diffuse patterns that are "replaced by more specialized functions" (p. 255). Katz and Kahn note that "social organizations move toward the multiplications and elaboration of roles with greater specialization of function" (p. 255).

Differentiation allows the organization to maintain a steady state. Von Bertalanffy discusses this in terms of primary and secondary regulation of the system:

> It can be shown that the primary regulations in organic systems, that is, those which are most fundamental and primitive in embryonic development as well as in evolution, are of such nature of dynamic interaction . . . . Superimposed are those regulations which we may call secondary, and which are controlled by fixed arrangements, especially of the feedback type. This state of affairs is a consequence of a general principle of organization which may be called progressive mechanization. At first, systems --- biological, neurological, psychological or social --- are governed by dynamic interaction of their components; later on, fixed arrangements and conditions of constraint are established which render the system and its parts more efficient, but also

gradually diminish and eventually abolish its equipotentiality (Emery, 1969, p. 94).

It is the secondary regulations that von Bertalanffy speaks of that are of interest for this review. Referring to policy analysis, the nature of the secondary regulations determines not only the level of efficiency of the organization or institution but also the ability of that organization to respond effectively to change in its environment.

The final general characteristic of open systems that Katz and Kahn speak of is *equifinality*. This principle states that "a system can reach the same final state from differing initial conditions and by a variety of paths" (p. 256). In organization theory terms this means that there is no one best way, a phrase left over from the scientific management school of the early 1900s.

In recent years many administrative theorists have strived to apply systems concepts to management. However, policy research in law enforcement has traditionally taken a mechanistic approach focusing on the law, structure, and the institution. The behavior of the human actors is what can be categorized as the missing element from many of these studies. Laws neither make nor enforce themselves, and legal research has a tendency to camouflage and obscure the behavior of the actors in the system. Systems theory may still be evolving, but as pointed out by Kast and Rosensweig (1972), it "provides a relief from the limitations of more mechanistic approaches and a rationale for rejecting principles based on relatively closed-system thinking" (p. 447).

General Systems Theory and Police Policy

Munro (1979) insists that general systems theory, combined with role analysis, has the potential for providing the behavioral context for structural-legal policy issues. He describes two aspects of specific use to policy analysis that involve role set and organizational roles. As shown in Figure 1, Munro portrays a generalized role set for a chief of police with respect to the policy issue of police discretion as it might apply in a use of force incident. The role set is composed of all roles that are directly tied together. Note that the solid line arrows indicate intra-organization members, and the dashed arrows indicate extra-organization members.

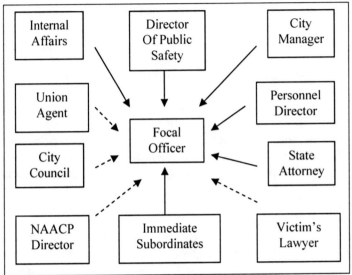

Figure 1. Generalized role set in a use of force incident.
Source: Munro, J. L., *Administrative Behavior and Police Organization*
(1974). Cincinnati, OH: W. H. Anderson Co.

Munro is able to illustrate how the role set transcends simple organizational or agency boundaries, and that it involves substantial non-organizational members. Of course, the composition of the role set can vary depending on the policy issue under consideration.

In addition, the factors that influence the behavior of the policy maker (focal officer) must be taken into consideration. Of course, some of the most important role inputs for many criminal justice policy decisions come from legal and organizational factors. Katz and Kahn use a model in which they identify three important modifying elements.

First are the attributes of the person being examined such as; behavioral preferences, defense mechanisms, race, age, and sex variables. Next are the policymaker's interpersonal relations, which include but are not limited to, quality, content, and frequency of interaction among the roles of a specific situational role set. Finally, is the actual behavior of the policymaker, which is fed back to the role set and consequently causes the role senders to modify their role-expectations.

As pointed out by Katz and Kahn, the primary mission of an organization as perceived by its leaders will normally provide evidence of the organizational functions. In spite of this, mission statements, organizational reports, and value statements can be misleading. Such statements, while not intentionally deceptive, may idealize, distort, or even omit essential aspects of the functioning of the organization. In fact, agreement about the mission of the organization between leaders and members may routinely be in dispute, and law enforcement is no exception.

Dealing with policy analysis while utilizing a general systems approach, Munro claims that system boundaries must be determined. He refers to the action boundary, which is essentially the point in social space within which implementation and operational behaviors are taking place. Another boundary, policy-analytical, represents that portion of social space within which policy questions are being determined and/or analyzed. The precision of the boundaries definition is dependent on the policy in question, the complexity of the behavioral and structural-legal situation, and the sophistication of the research methods.

The issues of boundaries, role sets, organizational factors, and legal parameters can make for an extraordinarily complex scheme. Munro states that there is a way to work through the confusion in what von Bertalanffy (1968) calls "the establishment of leading parts, that is, components dominating the behavior of the system" (p. 213). Von Bertalanffy believed that the leading parts exert a "trigger causality" in that a small change in such parts may, by way of amplification mechanisms, cause large changes in the total system. In this way a hierarchic order of parts or processes could be established. Munro feels that creating measures of the frequency, strength, and salience of system transactions can easily identify the leading parts of the system (p. 10). He gives examples of amplification mechanisms such as, local matching funds to attract federal funding, or federal funds utilized to induce local institutions into changing programs and processes.

Once the system boundaries have been established, then the role set for a particular policy issue can be identified. A primary role set might focus on a police chief, city manager, union leader, or even a committee. Identification of the role set (like the one used in Figure 1) will allow the policy analyst to determine the leading parts of that particular system. An example for police arrest procedures could encompass state statutes regulating such action, the county attorney responsible for reviewing possible criminal charges, and department policy. Munro states that these leading parts could then be analyzed as the "focal person." The process would then be used to focus on different leading actors, which produces a rotating behavioral matrix. As the analyst goes through the policy process (i.e., identification, setting agenda, formulation, implementation, etc.), a different set of leading parts is analyzed based on their importance and strategies are developed.

Influences on Governance

Public administrators and political scientists have investigated the ways in which the political, professional, and technical characteristics of public organizations influence the making and execution of government policy. To do so requires identification of a level, or levels, of analysis. Some research focuses on the individual, whereas other studies are concerned with groups or the organization as a whole. The structures, hierarchies, and environment of the organization tend to increase the complexity of such analyses. For example, the hierarchical structure that occurs when individuals are nested within work groups and work groups within departments results in three possible levels of analysis (individual, group, organization). Another example involves the organizational environment. Most scholars agree that there are two basic types of environment (internal and external), and that there are three specific areas (task, institutional, and environmental-ecological) that relate to the basic types. These topics do not, however, constitute unrelated or mutually exclusive categories. The areas of analysis described can relate or overlap in numerous ways.

It is beyond the scope of this study to provide a detailed analysis on the competing demands from all the various groups that take an interest in police policy in our pluralist society; nonetheless, a brief examination of some of the more discernible interests is necessary. The environments of the public, our political system, administration, the media, the justice system, unions, and even the police themselves will be reviewed from the organizational impact that such interactions have that are constantly attempting to influence the policymaking process.

Police Culture

Policing, particularly because it is a twenty-four-hour-a-day identity, generates powerfully distinctive ways of looking at the world. These include cognitive and behavioral responses which, when taken together, may be said to constitute "a working personality" (Skolnick and Fyfe, 1993). No matter how many warnings may be issued by superiors about limitations on the use of force, or how much persuasion is made that policing is a profession, police training continually reminds recruits that coercive power is a central feature of police life. Those who are being policed do not distinguish among blue uniforms. All cops come to be defined as brutal, and thus appropriate targets for retaliation. Hated cops are not safer cops. William Ker Muir (1977) was the first police scholar to call attention to the paradoxes of coercive power. He saw how police who are gifted with maturity, empathy, and interpersonal skills could escape from the trap of relying on the threat of force.

It has been suggested that the best ways of minimizing violence between police and citizens is to harness and articulate the overlooked expertise of street cops, the people most qualified by experience – and necessity – to prescribe guidelines for averting bloodshed (Toch, Grant, & Galvin, 1975).

Even police officers themselves have become a source of data for police abuse. In the Bayley and Mendelsohn study, 100 officers were surveyed (1969). Researchers report that 53 percent of the officers acknowledged that they had witnessed an "incident that someone might consider to constitute police brutality" (p. 128). Twenty-seven percent of the officers admitted that in fact they had observed incidents that involved excessive use of force. In another study of a small southern city in the late 1970s, Barker (1978) found that on average, officers reported that 40 percent of their fellow officers used excessive force on a prisoner. The only other misconduct by police in the Barker study found to be as prevalent was sleeping on duty.

It is hard to think of any hierarchical organization in which the lowest-level employees routinely exercise such great discretion with such little opportunity for objective review. This is no meaningless anomaly. Trying to adapt street-level officers' great discretion into the lowest level of a military organizational style has resulted in the creation of elaborate police rulebooks that pretend to be definitive but provide little meaningful guidance for police officers. Hard and fast rules are viable in mechanical work situations, but they are of little assistance in dealing with the fluid discretionary situations that are the core of police work (Skolnick and Fyfe, 1993). Michael Lipsky (1980) noted that the accountability of "street level bureaucrats" such as police officers, teachers, and social workers is tenuous at best. Since they are rarely dependent upon the approval and satisfaction of their clients, they are inclined to misperceive client needs, motives and capabilities.

It is extremely difficult for police who work in inner-city slums to overcome the distrust and resentment of the very people who most need good police service. Where police departments make no effort to overcome those barriers or, worse, where they fail to acknowledge that they exist, and cling instead to some simplistic version of color-blind professionalism, latent resentments become open antagonism. It is hypocritical for police who work in cities where social class and race make so much difference in everybody's life to claim that they can perform their work uninfluenced by such considerations.

In a study conducted by George Felkenes (1993) of the Claremont Graduate School, it was reported that regardless of race and gender, virtually all Los Angeles police officers see themselves as detached from the public, at war with the press, and under-appreciated and disliked by an ungrateful public. As Felkenes suggests, the organization apparently has hardened the newcomers' views far more than they have mellowed the department:

> The officers do appear to take on an attitude that can be described as "cloning," in which a diverse group is so indoctrinated into the police culture that they become all but indistinguishable (p. 138.)

Skolnick and Fyfe (1993) argue that police who ride in patrol cars, especially two-person cars, become rather self-contained and remote, isolating themselves from the people they serve. This detachment does nothing to enhance the public safety perception of citizens. While officer safety concerns and union involvement often promote the two-person car strategy, research suggests that such a strategy is far less productive than solo units and no more likely to reduce injuries for officers (Conkrite, 1983). In addition, two-person patrol cars are no more effective in catching criminals or reducing crime.

This culture of traditional policing has been the target of sociologists trying to explain the fundamental problem of police abuse (Klockars, 1985). A prelude to the abuse of authority and force tends to occur when police develop deviant visions of their work. In one such example the Christopher Commission (1991) identified what it referred to as a "siege mentality," in which the police place a superior emphasis of crime control over crime prevention and isolate themselves from the communities and people they serve. The organization exacerbates the problem by rewarding officers for the number of calls they handle and arrests they make.

The other is the "Dirty Harry" vision, which rationalizes vigilante justice. The "Dirty Harry" dilemma, named by sociologist Carl B. Klockers, who got it from the 1971 Warner Brothers film, dramatized a fundamental problem for police. A morally good end can utilize whatever means necessary to accomplish the objective. For police executives this aggressive and proactive way of doing business was accepted as the most cost-effective deterrent to potential offenders (Skolnick & Fyfe, 1993). In tolerating such excesses the hope was that the sensational headlines and television news stories that followed would encourage criminals to take their business elsewhere.

As police executives began to learn that the styles mentioned above were in reality very costly, and did little to impact the crime problem, they moved to change the police culture. In fact, during the 1970s and 1980s, the police argued there was little they could do about crime, that rates were determined by demographics and social conditions. With the help of groups such as the Police Foundation and the Police Executive Research Forum (PERF), a more educated, innovative brand of cop was beginning to develop.

Goldstein (1990) believes that a significant goal for present day police executives should be to develop their departments' organizational culture and rhythm to reflect varying community values, and the understanding that their officers need to behave predictably and in accordance with their training. Today's administrators should strive for a diverse department, but they must also recognize that it should not matter whether the cop who shows up in response to a citizen's call for help is black or white, male or female, fundamentalist or atheist. These administrators should seek diversity at the broadest level; yet maintain consistency at the one-to-one level of the cop on the street.

Political Environment

Smith (1960) discusses the situation of policing presented in the United States and claims it is not altogether unique. In other parts of the world, under all types of governments, police forces are never quite free of the taint of corruption. Nowhere has there been a successful repression or suppression of all criminal acts, or a large portion of effective prosecutions in proportion to total offenses reported. In addition, Smith argues that many prosecutions and definitions of criminal acts are deeply rooted in political manipulations of various kinds.

Politics is often seen as exalting personal loyalty or partisan interests above the public good rather than as the democratic political process that provides needed governance in our lives. Add to this adverse climate for police a political atmosphere that greatly influences their actions. These political reactions can involve delimiting the power and authority of the organization, and refocusing resources on lower priorities. For example, if a situation involving force causes a highly charged public response, politicians may react based on their immediate political needs, instead of a logical and evenhanded evaluation of the merits of the incident. This may result in pressure for inappropriate action, such as restricting patrols in high density minority neighborhoods.

McLaughlin (1992) outlines several societal and legal conditions that significantly impact and present challenges to the way police do their jobs. He argues that there are four societal conditions that are constantly in flux and acting on each other: a liberal democracy, clashing cultures, the underclass, and political motivations. This can cause the police to find themselves receiving inconsistent signals from their elected officials. Further compounding this ambiguity are legal considerations. McLaughlin outlines five different types of legal and quasi-legal scrutiny that may be applied when an officer is involved in a faulty arrest situation: federal criminal law, federal civil law, state criminal law, state civil law, and departmental regulations. However, in the case of a person assaulting a police officer that suspect is commonly charged once and adjudicated once.

Political manipulation and law enforcement seem always to have been closely associated in the United States. Even during the larger stages of the colonial period, when our democratic patterns were just beginning to take form, there were traces of this alliance. Colonial sheriffs exercised a large political influence, their powers in the conduct of elections were frequently abused for partisan advantage, and the collection of taxes, often entrusted to them by law, was sometimes employed for political as well as personal ends. With the appearance of cities and great metropolitan areas the effect of such influences was magnified. (Leonard & More, 2000)

There can be no doubt that the greatest handicap of modern police administration is derived from partisan politics. Its pressure is applied under all systems and always affects management. No system is entirely free from it. In most countries it is exercised chiefly by the ruling class, and thereby becomes completely identified with police administration. The result may be an efficient though irresponsible police machine (Swanson, Territo & Taylor, 1988.)

Here in the United States there is no such well-defined pattern. According to Smith (1960), the political influences are so numerous and so varied that their effect is "kaleidoscopic." Sometimes they are so diametrically opposed that they tend to offset each other. Usually, however, either some one political interest is able to dominate or conflicting partisan interests are reconciled. The result is quickly reflected in leadership of poor quality, low standards of personnel management, inferior service, and a general decline in police prestige.

Ultimate control in local government is normally exerted through the ballot box, but efforts to protect the police from partisan political influence have, in many jurisdictions, made the police immune from the local election processes. Early efforts to assure popular control of the police did include provisions in some cities for the chief of police to be elected. In others, the police were made responsible to the local legislative body. It became quickly apparent, however, that such direct control led to a pattern of incompetence, lax enforcement, and the improper use of police authority. Elected office holders dictated the appointment and assignment of personnel, exchanged immunity from enforcement for political favors, and, in some cities, made use of the police to assist in the winning of elections (Swanson et al. 1988).

In more recent times there has been a continuing effort to comprise the need for popular control with the need for a degree of operating independence in order to avoid the undesirable practices that have generally resulted from direct political control. Election and city council supervision of the police function gradually gave way to the establishment of administrative boards, variously constituted, in an effort to assure both independence and some semblance of civilian control.

These organizational patterns have, in turn, often led to an obscuring of responsibilities, resulting in a swing back to more direct control in the form of a movement for the appointment of a single executive, directly answerable to the elected mayor or, more recently, to a city manager who in turn is responsible to a city council. Variations of each of these arrangements, including some attempts at state control, continue to this day, with periodic shifting from one organizational pattern to another in response to a community's conclusion that its police force has too much or too little independence.

The record of involvement by elected officials in police operations, to the detriment of both the efficiency and effectiveness of the police establishment, has had a lasting and somewhat negative impact on the lines of control between the citizenry and the police. In cities in which the desire to isolate the police from political interference led to the adoption of special organizational patterns, the change in some instances has had the effect of making the police impervious to citizen demands of a legitimate nature (Kerstetter, 1985).

It may be helpful, in the long-range interest of law enforcement, to involve local officials in the process of developing enforcement policies, particularly those that have an impact upon a broad segment of the community. If, for example, a police agency were to adopt a policy to govern individual officers in deciding what to do with the down-and-out drunk, it would seem appropriate and helpful to report that policy to the mayor and city council in order to see whether there is opposition from the elected representatives. Where the issue is significant enough, a public hearing may serve to give an indication of the community response to the particular policy being proposed. Although this involvement of city government may give rise to concern over "political influence," the risk of improper influence is minimized by the fact that the involvement is open to view. The vice of political influence of an earlier day was that it tended to be of a personal nature and was secretive. The consequence is that we are now in a period of uncertainty as to the best relationship between police and city government, and the issue has been aggravated by the situation of unrest in large urban areas.

Administration

Many, if not most, police chief executives express serious concerns with the authority a political chief executive (mayor or city manager) exerts or attempts to exert over their responsibilities. The suggestion is that the political officials are involved in matters that should not fall within their purview. However, city and town managers represent much of what is associated with the progressive and reform origins of public administration – professional management, merit civil service, public service distribution without favoritism, uncorrupt relations with vendors and contractors, efficiency, economy, and above all, a firewall between city politics and city administration (Frederickson, 1997).

The council-manager style of government represents what Frederickson refers to as the "pure form" of the policy-administration dichotomy. In the past, managers were mainly concerned with economic development issues. Now, the issues of neighborhoods, responsiveness to communities, and political, economic, and social leaders have moved to the forefront of concern.

Frederickson (1997) believes that the city manager form of government fosters professionalization. By placing full responsibility on the city manager, the belief is that only capable competent individuals would be placed as department heads. For most towns and cities, the position of police chief would be a critical concern to the manager. By having the chief directly responsible to the city manager, political interference from legislative and political executives of government would be reduced to a minimum. This may be more of an idealistic approach than a reality.

Administrators of public agencies have been asked for some time now to take note of public sentiment and political concerns. Frederickson (1997), in his chapter titled "*Pushing Things Up to Their First Principles,*" discusses the move from task, domain, and level to the demand for responsibility, accountability, and service (p. 232). In today's society administrators and executives, to include police executives, are being asked to take a hard look at their entire organization, realizing that they will be operating with fewer resources while simultaneously being asked to provide the public with increased services. The focus of accountability is to the citizenry.

Unfortunately, accountability to the community has been extremely limited under the traditional style of policing. The American criminal justice system has done an eminently poor job of establishing clear, enduring, precise guidelines for police officers, especially when it comes to such areas as discretionary decision making by police (McLaughlin, 1992). If American Policing is to enjoy the label of professionalism it only makes sense that one of the most contentious issues of law enforcement, the use of discretion, require established guidelines and training. Relevant to policy enforcement is the extent to which complaints of policy violations are scrutinized and violations are punished. The police chief, who has a tendency to be insulated from the outside world by hordes of aides and layers of bureaucracy, must focus an institutional effort around one job: that of the police officer closest to the communities. Everything else should be secondary according to Albert Reiss (1985).

However, as police departments move into the realm of "community-policing," Goldstein (1990) cautions police executives against relying on such a philosophy to be a cure-all for organizational deficiencies in poor citizen relations. He maintains that research and problem solving must become an integral part of the policy process, much more than has been done in the past. By making research a core technology of policing, Goldstein believes that many of law enforcement's problems will be easier to control. Such research would require police organizations to evaluate their function, accountability, and their relationship to the community, rather than what they can do about the crime problem.

This raises a fundamental issue for police administrators, that being identification of the core function of the organization. Some researchers and sociologists feel that a move to order-maintenance should be the central function of the police as opposed to crime suppression, while others seriously disagree (see e.g., Kelling et al., 2000; Klockars, 1985). Order maintenance is an active role by the police in the suppression of a whole range of citizen behaviors and activities that has the potential for serious abuse. The most telling example of success involves the New York police department and their program of "Compstat."

During the 1970s and 1980s, the New York police themselves argued there was little they could do about crime, that rates were determined by demographics and social conditions. However, during the 1990s Commissioner William Bratton and his successor, Howard Safir, created a model of policing that is important for two reasons. First, the drop in homicides in New York went from 1,946 in 1993, to

983 in 1996. This accounts for more than a 50% drop in homicides, and accounted by itself for a 20% drop nationwide. Second was the level of accountability placed on department administrators.

Bratton put primary responsibility in the hands of his 76 precinct commanders and then held them personally accountable for reducing crime in their neighborhoods. To facilitate this program, he used a process called "Compstat," for "compare statistics." The NYPD can now plot each reported crime on a color map that gives police a more sophisticated understanding of crime trends, patterns, and "hot spots." In twice-weekly strategy meetings Bratton weeded out commissioners that were weak performers; replacing half his precinct commanders within a year (Witkin, 1998).

However, many experts also attribute part of New York's success to Bratton's focus on arrest for nuisance crimes – street prostitution, public urination, or blaring boomboxes. Bratton consciously took to heart the "Broken Windows" theory postulated by James Q. Wilson and criminologist George Kelling. Published in a 1982 *Atlantic Monthly* article, Wilson and Kelling raised the issue of minor offenses and their link to the fear of crime, serious crime, and urban decay. Although this article remains controversial, especially in light of New York City's 1990s crime decline, it nevertheless convinced policy makers and police that citizen concerns for problems ranging from graffiti to aggressive panhandling to street prostitution had to be taken seriously. This was necessary to improve the quality of neighborhood life and to improve the quality of the relationship between citizens and police, especially in poor and minority communities.

The strongest criticism of such order maintenance strategies is that it brings into question some basic issues of liberty, equity, due process, individual self-expression, and privacy. In fact, since the initial numbers showing dramatic decreases in crime during the 1990s in New York city, critics have questioned the increase in "Gestapo" tactics by police, which they believe leads to unconscionable use of force by the police. These same critics point to the case in which four NYPD officers shot an unarmed Black man, Amadou Diallo, numerous times for pulling his wallet out to provide identification.

But Kelling argues that the priority for time and resources in order-maintenance may provide superior opportunities for making a difference in the lives of citizens. A police department that places order-maintenance uppermost in its priorities will judge patrol officers less by their arrest records and more by their ability to keep the peace on their beat. This will require that sergeants and other supervisory personnel concern themselves more with how the patrol officers function in family fights, teenage disturbances, street-corner brawls, and civil disorders, and less with how well they take reports at the scene of a burglary or how many traffic tickets they issue during a tour of duty.

Public Environment

The growth of police systems in this country has been one of extraordinary rapidity. Police service in the United States has never really enjoyed an opportunity for orderly and consistent development (Goldstein, 1990). From the earliest days of modern police forces, and down through the years that have followed, police have been the object of attack by press and pulpit, bench and bar, civic and commercial associations, labor leaders, professional politicians, ambitious office seekers, reformers, and criminals. With so many social elements joining in the attack, the charges have naturally ranged between some rather wide extremes. Police have been denounced as relentless man hunters, as oppressors of the weak and helpless, and as the tools of sinister influences and interests. They have also been described as largely ineffective agencies that fail to realize their objectives and in any case cost too much (Smith, 1960).

The kinds of police activities apparently best adapted to suppressing street crime – intensive patrols, close surveillance of "suspicious" persons, frequent street stops of pedestrians and motorists, and so on – are precisely those most likely to place the police in conflict with important segments of the community – primarily with persons who because of their age, race, or social class have been regarded as most likely to commit criminal acts. In short, in the one aspect of law enforcement where there may be opportunities for substantial deterrence, the police are obliged to act in a way which, like their actions in order-maintenance situations, is most likely to bring them into conflict with the citizen (Wilson, 1968).

In a democratic government, the basic principle that administration be responsive to public control holds especially true for police administrators. This is because of the unique and special powers with which the police are entrusted. However, Kelling et al. (2000), explain that pressures and controls by various special interest groups can act to impede such standards. These groups may attempt illegitimate controls through the beat officer, police executive, the Mayor or City Council, or even a combination of these. The failure of responsible citizens to get involved with the affairs of local government can exacerbate the damage done by such special interest groups. This is not to say that there have not been legitimate attempts to make inroads into police policy by the community. Take for example, civilian review.

In October 1958, Philadelphia became the first city in the nation to establish a civilian review board. The Police Advisory Board (PAB), created by an executive order of Mayor Richardson Dilworth, was authorized to accept citizen complaints of police misconduct and, after study, to make recommendations to the commissioner concerning the innocence, guilt, and possible punishment of officers' involved (Pogrebin & Regoli, 1986).

Nonetheless, a renewed campaign against the PAB gathered momentum in August 1964, when three days of rioting and looting in North-Central Philadelphia caused property damage estimated at $3,000,000 and injuries to one hundred policemen and more than two hundred civilians (Lohman & Misner, 1966). The new lodge president explained the connection between the civilian board and the riot in these blunt words: "If it hadn't been for the P.A.B. we would have grabbed them (the rioters) and if they resisted hit them with our black jacks" (Pogrebin & Regoli, 1986, p. 214). The rioting persisted for nearly four days, F.O.P. leaders claimed, only because Philadelphia police officers were reluctant to use adequate force for fear of being brought before the board.

It is not unusual for law enforcement agencies to express considerable resistance to citizen involvement in the policymaking process. The loss of autonomy is a serious concern by police executives, who view such attempts as an attack on their ability to lead and an impediment to effective policing. Police administrators argue that it has taken considerable time in this country to remove partisan political interference from law enforcement, and public involvement in police policy will leave them exposed to the most vocal and disruptive segments of society (Andrews, 1985). Of course, opponents dispute this claim and point out that our country was founded on citizen participation, and that the community should be part of the decision making process. In allowing such participation the belief is that a broader base of support would exist for the acceptance and support of enforcement policies.

Accountability of the police is not just a political issue. Various studies have attempted to survey citizens to determine whether they have been the subject of police misconduct, have seen police misconduct, or heard about police misconduct (Skolnick and Fyfe, 1993). However, many of these studies rely on the subjects' interpretations of what defines "misconduct." Traditionally, negative experiences with police tend to be much higher among minority citizens than those of Caucasian descent. Such studies should not be dismissed solely on the perception of flawed interpretivism, but should be scrutinized as to whether the findings represent an objective reality or one that is socially constructed.

One attempt to address citizens' concerns in this area is a mechanism referred to as the citizen complaint procedure. The process allows citizens the opportunity to lodge a formal complaint if they feel that they have been the victim of police misconduct. Such a complaint initiates an investigation into the actions of the officer/s involved. The goal is to increase public confidence and increase the level of professionalism of the police department. Unfortunately, there seems to be wide variation among departments with regard to the process of receiving complaints and how such complaints are processed (Dugan & Breda, 1991; Kerstetter, 1985; Pate & Fridell, 1993). Predictably, it is the complaint process that comes under review and scrutiny when the police come under fire for misconduct. Detailed procedures on the complaint process that have been subject to review by the community can help to alleviate such problems.

No matter how detailed the complaint procedure, it may not address the issue of public concern about the police "policing themselves," or the disparity of minority perceptions about police misconduct. In a survey of 806 Denver, Colorado residents done in 1966, respondents were asked about experiences with "police brutality" (Bayley and Mendelsohn, 1969). Only 4 percent of Caucasians claimed to have experienced police brutality compared with 9 percent of African Americans, and 15 percent of citizens with Spanish surnames. According to Bayley and Mendelsohn, 30 percent of the African Americans reported that they had heard of charges of police brutality from friends compared to 4 percent of Caucasians and 12 percent of Hispanics.

Complaints alleging police misconduct may relate to an isolated incident involving the actions of a specific officer or may relate to a formal or informal practice generally prevailing throughout a department. However, the citizen complaint process, like the civil action, is typically limited, in its effect, to the specific case that is subject to review. Whatever the method for conducting an investigation, there is no evidence that the complaint procedure has generally served as a significant vehicle for the critical evaluation of existing police practices and the development of more adequate departmental policies.

In some areas of governmental activity, there is increasing utilization of citizen advisory committees as a way of involving members of the community in the policymaking process. In some cases, the group may be advisory only, the governmental agency being free to accept or reject its advice. In other instances, the group is official and policies are cleared through the committee as a regular part of the policymaking process. The advantages of both methods are that they serve as an inducement for the police administrator to articulate important policies, to formulate them, and to subject them to discussion in the advisory group. How effective this is depends upon the willingness of the group and the police administrator to confront the basic law-enforcement policy issues rather than being preoccupied with the much easier questions of the mechanics of running the department. Where there is a commitment to exploring basic enforcement policy questions, the citizens' advisory group or policymaking board has the advantage of involving the community in the decision-making process, thus giving a broader base than would otherwise exist for the acceptance and support of enforcement policies.

The basic need can be stated briefly, though at some risk of oversimplification. It is for giving police policymaking greater visibility, so that the community knows the problems and current police solutions.

The Media

Rarely does a major piece of police work receive the accolade of general approval. It may even be doubted whether any single instance of police action has ever been wholly satisfactory to all concerned, since an otherwise perfect example of police work is likely to be viewed with something less than enthusiasm by the thwarted or apprehended offender. The environment in which police must do their work is therefore certain to be unfavorable. Good immediate results are difficult to secure and may bring new and unexpected favors into operation. The chain of circumstances thus forged proves a burden to even the best police organizations (Skolnick & Fyfe, 1993).

Most likely there is not a police administrator that exists that does not understand that the media can be a powerful friend or an overwhelming foe when it comes to the operation of his/her organization. Significant factors to the police-media relationship include attitudes, policies, and working relationships between the two entities. No matter how good the relationship is, conflicts will occur between the police and the media, and it usually emanates from events surrounding a major crime or unusual occurrence (Vance, 1997).

The media process and how it presents public perceptions and changes and revises our framework of meaning in the public domain, is consequential in our social life (Altheide, 1996). In a culture that has been recorded and replayed more than any other, the electronic media in the United States presents a significant challenge to the police executive. Even the most carefully formulated editorial policies are often offset by news policy deliberately designed to generate ratings. Those who determine editorial policies themselves have been misled occasionally into condemning the police when they were right and praising them when they were wrong. So there are few influences at work for instruction of the public in the harsh realities of police duty and in the more or less objective standards of police service (Smith, 1960).

Educating the public on the realities and complexities of the police organization is a difficult task at best, and almost impossible without the media. Some of that understanding can come about through scholarly research, and indeed, starting in the 1960s, a substantial literature emerged, from both scholarly and task force inquiries (see e.g., Davis, 1975; Goldstein, 1977; Muir, 1977; Neiderhoffer 1976; Rubinstein, 1973; Skolnick & Fyfe, 1993; and J.Q. Wilson, 1968).

Unfortunately, the average citizen is not exposed to such research, and typically draws his/her conclusions, aside from direct contact, from the mass media. And few newspapers or television stations encourage reporters to delve deeply into the structures and processes of policing in this day and age of "sound bites." According to Skolnick and McCoy (1984), the public is too often exposed to reportage about events associated with policing and too little introduced to the institution of policing and the administrative issues implicit in the policing process.

Unions

Police executives and public administrators are quickly learning that they must provide participation with employee organizations in law enforcement when determining police policy. Though the policymaking process has been broadened to allow for input from line officers through formal and informal negotiation between department and association leaders, the major struggle over policy still involves only police officers. Indeed, the closed nature of the police system, which has long been a concern of citizens and critics of the police, has been strengthened by the combination of the commitment to professionalize American police and the success of the efforts to organize them. The efforts to take the police out of politics and politics out of policing has given credible justification for such a closed system; helping to ensure that police policymaking remains the exclusive prerogative of police executives. Administrators have been nervously resistive in their sharing of control over policy; yet, have found employee organization leaders outspoken and forceful allies in fighting to retain departmental autonomy in accountability procedures and other policymaking.

Such an alliance may not come without a downside. As cities run into revenue concerns and are unable to make monetary concessions, police and municipal management representatives may look to alternative compromises. In a number of large cities unions have been successful in chipping away at prerogatives long considered to be the province of the police chief. Policymaking, misconduct investigations, work force deployment and many other areas are being given serious consideration in union bargaining tactics. The specific concessions yielded to the unions, sometimes by city labor lawyers who lack even basic familiarity with the complexities of urban policing, occasionally reverse hard-won reforms of prior generations of police executives.

However, the contrast of union leaders is evident as they point to the politicized, elitist treatment of the industry by its own administrators. They argue that management fails to provide recognition or support to the line officer and the vast discretionary powers that are placed onto them. Add to that the resistance by management to involve line officers' with their street expertise in the policymaking process and you have a sizeable obstacle to improved policing (Dodenhoff, 1985).

If there is a middle ground where management and labor seem to come together, it concerns the threat to police power. Studies have shown that police officers are especially responsive to attacks on their authority (LaFave, 1965; Toch, 1965; Westley, 1970). The low estimate police have of public support, their sensitivity to the deference shown police authority, wide discretion in police work situations (Wilson, 1968) and unattainable role expectations (Manning, 1980) make police officers insecure bureaucrats, and civilian review boards attractive issues for leaders, or would be leaders, of police associations to dramatize and exploit.

Another issue involving the unions and police administration deals with discipline. Police executives have recently met with increased resistance in attempting to discipline subordinates for misconduct or illegal behavior. Most urban departments come under the municipal civil service regulations, which tend to restrict reform efforts of police commanders (President's Commission, 1967, p. 210). In the past few years, local police organizations have displayed significant success in coming to the defense of police who have been accused of corrupt activities, thus preventing punitive action toward those officers.

Judicial Review

Judicial review should not be construed as a review of department administrative policy. Such a review may seem appropriate, but in reality is most unlikely when it is a criminal case charged against a suspect. While this type of judicial process may examine the actions of the individual officer, the focus tends to be that of the suspect actions. Judges seldom ask for and, as a consequence, are not informed as to whether there is a current administrative policy. And, if there is one, they seldom ask whether the officer's conduct in the particular case conformed to or deviated from the policy. As a result, police are not encouraged to articulate and defend their policy; the decision of the trial judge is not even communicated to the police administrator; and the prevailing police practice often continues unaffected by the decision of the trial judge (Pogrebin & Regoli, 1986). Many times police tend to ignore all of the decisions, rationalizing that it is impossible to conform to conflicting mandates. While increasing attention has been given to minimizing sentencing disparity through such devices as sentencing institutes, no similar attention has been given to disparity in the supervision of police practices.

Hall (1999) argues that even the effectiveness of the exclusionary rule is limited by the fact that it deals only with police practices leading up to prosecution.   Many highly sensitive and important police practices are confined to the street and are not reflected in prosecuted cases.   In the unusual case where an individual is able to successfully gain a money judgment in an action brought against a police officer or governmental unit, this does not necessarily result in the reevaluation of departmental policy or practice.

In situations of criminal cases charged against police officers, the attention still seems to center around the actions of the individual officer and not policy issues. However, in recent years the U.S. Justice Department has taken a more active role in "pattern and practice" cases which lead to consent decrees.[2]   As recently as 1981 the Justice Department was obtaining convictions in about one hundred police brutality cases every year (FBI, Civil Rights Program, 1997).   The Justice Department asserts that department and city size along with number of arrests was not a predictor of the number of civil rights complaints received.

Interestingly, the Independent Commission of the Los Angeles Police Department (1991) found no evidence that either the degree of legitimate force or improper violence used by police in the course of their work had any effect on crime or public safety.

Criminal judicial review at trial is typically initiated by the state or city through a prosecutor, and may only provide a narrow focus for the citizen involved to question department policy. On the other hand, civil judicial review has grown exponentially over the past two decades, and has become a serious concern for city and police administrators.

The liability for personal injuries or property damage is generally handled under applicable state laws. However, Section 1983 of The Civil Rights Act, Title 42 United States Code, is the section most commonly used when an officer has deprived someone of their civil rights (Hall, 1999). These rights include the right not to have life, liberty, or property taken without due process of law.

---

[2]Consent decrees are contractual agreements in which a law enforcement agency avoids federal litigation.

In a case that is unrelated to police conduct, the Supreme Court opened the door for a boom in civil rights litigation involving police actions. In *Monell v. Department of Social Services of the City of New York* (1978), Mrs. Monell applied for maternity leave and was subsequently forced to resign by her boss. In this case the Supreme Court established a major legal principle:

> Where a representative of an official agency (Monell's supervisor) violates an individual's Constitutional rights as a result of the agency's official custom and practice, the agency as well as the individual employee may be held liable (Hall, 1999).

At the time, the impact that this case would have on civil rights litigation involving the police was not fully realized. Just two years before Monell, in 1976, the U.S. Congress enacted a law that permitted judges to award successful plaintiffs "reasonable attorney's fees" as part of the costs, thereby, loosening the "purse strings" for such cases. Thus, Section 1983 litigation typically was no longer tied to the contingency fee system. Other Monell cases have held police agencies liable for inadequate policy and training regarding arrest, non-lethal force, strip searches, and vehicle pursuits (see e.g., *Canton v. Harris*, 1989).

Civil liability has always been of concern to police executives, but never to the extent that it is today. From 1986 through 1990, according to the Christopher Commission, Los Angeles paid in excess of $20 million in judgments, settlements, and jury verdicts in 300 suits against LAPD officers alleging excessive use of force. In what is now the infamous Rodney King case, Mr. King had sued the city seeking 15 million dollars in damages. After a three-week civil trial King received $3.8 million dollars tax-free award for medical bills, pain and suffering. It has been reported that the city attorney had originally suggested that an $800,000 settlement would have been appropriate. Other cases clearly illustrate a trend toward filing lawsuits against police officers.

In Phoenix, Arizona, a jury awarded $45 million to survivors of a double amputee who died while held with a neck hold when officers were trying to arrest him. Ultimately, attorneys negotiated a settlement amount to just over $5 million, but it was obvious that jurors in the case felt that the police should be held accountable to the citizens they serve (Leonard & More, 2000).

In 1997, Riverside County (CA) Sheriff's deputies beat two illegal immigrants after a freeway chase. Television news helicopters videotaped a deputy shoving a woman face-first on to the hood of a car, and then grabbing her by the hair and pulling her to the ground, where she was hit repeatedly. The man was also beaten. The two subjects split a $740,000 award.

However, when such a highly quantified cost-benefit analysis is used to measure police effectiveness, cash liability may be an inadequate corrective for police abuses. Even if half of the LAPDs $11.3 million liability bill in 1990 could be eliminated and converted to police salaries and personnel expenses, it would pay for only about seventy officers, less than a 1 percent increase in the department's personnel complement.

Thus, it appears that Monell, and more specifically section 1983 cases, brought on a one-on-one basis in the hope of winning money damages, will continue to serve as the most significant form of judicial oversight of the police (Skolnick & Fyfe, 1993). In general, however, it seems apparent that civil litigation is an awkward method of stimulating proper law enforcement policy. At most, it can furnish relief for the victim of clearly improper practices. To hold the individual officer liable in damages as a way of achieving systematic reevaluation of police practices seems neither realistic nor desirable.

The Police Role – A Theoretical Framework

The appropriate role of police is an area where there is some dissension among scholars; although, it is generally agreed that, in practice, police have multiple functions, many of which involve situations where no crime has occurred. The community, the law, and the policing organization provide the officer with rules, and these rules provide the officer with a sense of order —what the officer perceives as appropriate conduct (Ericson, 1982). Scholars suggest that police officers act on the basis of predispositions or overall orientations and these predispositions provide an interpretive framework in which the situational cues are evaluated (Wilson, 1968; Smith and Klein, 1983; Brown, 1988). Predispositions supply the officer with a repertoire of possible behavior and, from this collection, the officer selects an appropriate response to a specific situation. Even as much of the exposure of police work for officers contains similarities, there are profound differences in the way they respond. While there exists intuitive support for the connection between police discretion and organizational predispositions, little empirical research has been conducted to examine this issue.

Using Wilson's (1968) pioneering work of cross-classification of police agencies, police departments can be categorized under one of four groupings. These classifications revolve around the concepts of bureaucratization and professionalism (Smith and Klein, 1983). Wilson divides professional police agencies into service and legalistic styles, depending on their degree of bureaucratization. All nonprofessional departments are considered to operate under a watchman style, independent of their level of bureaucratization. Nonprofessional police agencies with shallow bureaucracies are labeled *fraternal*, while nonprofessional, bureaucratic police agencies are labeled *militaristic*. *Service* and *legalistic* departments are professional agencies that vary in terms of bureaucratization (see Figure 2).

Wilson argues that it is possible to determine whether top administrators in different types of police agencies hold different conceptions of the police role and have different expectations regarding appropriate police behavior. Smith and Klein (1983) found that such organizational properties did influence the probability of arrest, and more importantly, that certain situational variables on the decision to arrest were conditional on the organizational context in which the encounter occurred (p. 92). Thus, on one dimension there appears to be support for the thesis that differences in organizational ethos covary with structural characteristics of police agencies (i.e., bureaucratization and professionalism).

These suppositions are based on the premise that the exercise of discretion can be developed into an operational style preconditioned by the organization. Brown (1988) supports this by pointing out that discretion is value based and those values can be preconditioned by the organization (i.e., service, order maintenance, crime control), and such preconditions affect the arrest decision.

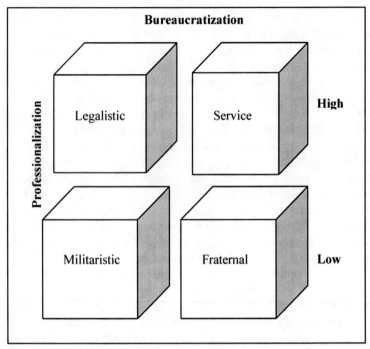

Figure 2. Classification of police departments by degree of
bureaucratization and professionalization.

   Control of official behavior under our system of government is
obviously a matter of legitimate public interest. But the police – and
especially police organizations – have come to bristle at the mere
mention of "controls" and, in some quarters, have gone so far as to
disclaim the right or competence of any external group to review police
conduct. Those who have taken this position ignore the fact that the
high value which our society places on individual rights requires that
there not only be limitations on the authority exercised by
governmental agencies, but that there be effective controls to assure
that such power is not exceeded or abused. The need for controls is
especially acute with regard to the police, for their authority – to arrest,
to detain, to search, and to use force – is unique among governmental
powers in the degree to which it is disruptive of freedom, invasive of

privacy, and the sudden and direct impact upon the individual (Smith, 1960).

It must be recognized that there has been a demonstrated need for control. Police understandably are sensitive to having documentation of abuse in years past cited to support the contention that the police of today are not to be trusted. Police administrators would argue that such practices as were described in the Wickersham Reports of the 1930s, for example, no longer exist. But the total record of police misconduct, scattered as it is, is too long and too recent to be ignored. Beyond this, it seems apparent that the very nature of the police function is likely to continue to give rise to situations in which individual officers may misuse their police powers. Considering these factors, it is not sufficient for the police to continue to respond to demands for the establishment of some form of controls, as has often been done in recent years, by citing the absence of any evidence of current abuse (Goldstein, 1977).

Another factor relates to the complexity of the police task and the conditions under which the police ordinarily function. Few citizens have a basis for understanding the environment in which a police officer assigned to patrol duties operates, unless their own work exposes them to the kinds of problems confronted by the police. Smith (1960) suggests that discussions relating to the problems inherent in controlling police behavior be undertaken with a full awareness of the need for considering the complex environment in which the police must usually function. The officers working in a congested section of a large city rush about the area to which they are assigned, caring for one incident after another. That officer's time is spent dealing with a concentration of social ills and with an infinite variety of situations requiring some form of action. Incidents considered as unusual occurrences by the average citizen constitute the officer's routine workload.

Most of the people with whom an officer is called upon to deal are in a highly emotional state. A large percentage are intoxicated. Many are abusive, and some are downright vicious. Speed in the making of decisions is often essential in order to avoid further harm to a victim, to safeguard the officer, or to prevent some form of mob action. Information required for the making of careful decisions is not always readily available, nor is it always possible to consult with superior officers when guidance is needed.

Smith argues that the police must maintain a system of internal discipline if the organization is to maintain legitimacy. While a monitoring agency outside the department may appeal to critics, it simply does not have the capacity to substitute for the numerous echelons of supervisory personnel that are required to provide on the spot direction. In fact, external controls could be found to diminish the desire and willingness of police administrators and their supervisors to elicit conformity to established standards of conduct from their subordinates.

Whether agreement can ever be reached on the internal or external oversight of law enforcement organizations, one thing is clear, research is beginning to look at the circumstances surrounding police abuses. However, as pointed out by Kerstetter (1985), it is precisely because the police are expected to detain and arrest violators of the law that inappropriate use of coercive force is the central problem of contemporary police misconduct. Any use of force by police must be constrained by the laws that they are bound to uphold. Any violation of those laws can be expected to undermine the public support and credibility that the police need to function effectively. Many times the mistakes made at these types of incidents result from the decision to arrest and a combination of cultural predisposition's and dysfunctional policies (Skolnick & Fyfe, 1993).

Among the most significant trends in the law enforcement field during the past decade has been the increase in efforts to subject the exercise of police authority to review and control from outside the police agency (see Pogrebin and Regoli, 1986; Pate and Fridell, 1993 and; Skolnick and Fyfe, 1993).

More recently, increased tensions experienced in some communities in the relationship between the police and local citizens have focused attention upon proposals for the establishment of civilian review boards to air complaints against police officers. Efforts on the part of the police to reduce such tensions have given rise to a third development – the establishment of new programs to improve police community relationships in which a special effort is made by the police to subject their operations to greater public view.

The findings of the Independent Commission on the Los Angeles Police Department (1991) confirm other findings of research in police abuses, that policies and procedures are insufficient in the absence of an administrative posture demanding compliance. The Commission determined that problems of police abuse had close ties to improper supervision along with poor management and leadership practices. This same theme was present in the American Civil Liberties Union 1991 release on *Police Brutality and its Remedies.* The ACLU maintains that police chiefs set the tone for a department and that their reaction has a big impact on future behavior.

Another problem, dealing with the reporting of arrests, is the accuracy of such incidents. It is very difficult to conduct field observations in anticipation of such situations, when such incidents are infrequent, especially if done from a covert research perspective. Archival records are typically voluntary and leave open the question of their accuracy and legitimacy, particularly in this day of a highly litigious society. From an organizational perspective, tactics that are improper, inappropriate, or ineffective are rarely the subject of departmental review and training (McLaughlin, 1992). Averted shootings, complaints not filed, and suspects that escape are normally not going to be reported unless the incident is brought to the forefront by an external source (i.e., media, videotape, or witness). Unfortunately, such data are forever lost for review.

However, even if the research community was in full agreement that police abuse involving such areas as false arrest and excessive force are rare events, it does not diminish the pervasive concern about the subject by present day society. This subject requires examination from multiple viewpoints. In fact, many police organizations have created policy or procedure, not based on empirical research, but on reaction by the public that, in turn, prompts public officials, city management and police executives to respond. Rising crime and even the fear of crime presents problems for police executives, but more often the abuse of authority and brutality by officers will shorten the career life of such administrators (Kelling, Wasserman, & Williams, 2000).

A link can be shown between administrative controls and the impact on officer behavior. What is less clear is the degree of impact that discipline, incentives, work controls, and the expectations of administrators and supervisors have on officer discretionary choices.

James Q. Wilson (1982) points out that the type of incident police officers confront may relate significantly to the ability of police administrators and supervisors' influence over police discretion. Clear choices, such as issuing a traffic citation for a serious violation, can be seriously ingrained into the police culture by an organization that emphasizes the need to cite and maintains audits to recap such productivity. However, a domestic disturbance may elicit only a prescription to "use common sense." The challenge is that complete conformity to policies and procedures in any organization is unlikely. To assume that police administrators shape police discretion is to assume that patrol officers not only understand what is wanted of them but that they willingly respond to organizational directives and the expectations of administrators. The difficulty for the police administrator is ensuring that officers do in fact what is desired by the organization.

The ability of top-level police administrators to control the exercise of discretion by patrol officers and the overall impact of administrative controls also depends on the size of the department. Direct control over subordinates is more difficult in large organizations, and the impact of hierarchichal controls may be more problematic (Child, 1973). In a small police department, by comparison, the proximity among administrators and patrol officers provides the access to an intimate knowledge of an officer's behavior that can replace or at least mediate formal controls. This proximity permits administrators to more directly and easily convey their expectations of the way events should be handled and to assure conformity.

Concept of Police Discretion

The use of administrative discretion, especially in the field of law enforcement, can have serious consequences. Even at the street level of police officer; varying degrees of action and inaction, the power to arrest or not arrest, who will benefit, who will be deprived, or how strictly the law will be enforced, are all acts of discretion that determine outcomes in individual cases. Does the exercise of such discretion seriously alter or contravene what the legislature had intended? Can discretion in the hands of police officers give them the power to reshape or otherwise modify policy decisions?

The range of discretionary choices open to a police officer may be highly structured and limited based on policy and oversight. Or they may have considerable freedom to decide when and how to act. Obviously, the greater the degree of autonomy a police officer has, the greater the potential for reshaping policy decisions through the exercise of discretion.

Many of these street-level bureaucrats interact directly with individual citizens and have substantial discretion in allocating assistance or imposing sanctions. They must continually make decisions, major and minor, about whether or not to apply the rules and how they should be interpreted in a specific case. Public-service workers make millions of decisions annually. These decisions can have an enormous impact on the lives of ordinary citizens.

The underlying principle of decision-making at this level involves the daily practice of street-level bureaucracy, which occurs despite the host of detailed rules and regulations that permeate most organizations. Reality is far too complicated to obtain an end-state without the use of discretionary powers by such street-level workers. Thus, they become more than the implementing agents of policy, but in fact, policy makers as well.

It is chiefly this actual decision-making power that traditionally has invoked great concern. What about the democratic control and accountability of all these self-appointed, nameless policy makers? How can they be prevented from developing into tiny oligarchs?

Historically, the police have asserted authority in many ways, often having nothing to do with arrest. Nonetheless, the arrest decision can have a significant and pervasive effect, not only on the arrestee, but also on the organization. Critical decision areas, such as the use of deadly force, have obvious impacts on the organization and have been heavily researched (Skolnick and Fyfe, 1993). However, the arrest decision, one that impacts the liberty of approximately 14 million people each year (FBI Uniform Crime Reports, 2000), seems to merit serious critical review. Critics claim that this decision (arrest) is largely ungoverned, and that police training goes a long way in teaching technique (i.e., approach, handcuffing, frisk, and so on), but does little to address the substantive issue of protecting citizen rights. The emphasis on mechanics and the neglect of substantive decisions are very similar to the state of police practices regarding deadly force thirty years ago.

Police executives' past efforts to control unnecessary discretion have had less than stellar results. Kelling (1999) argues that discretion in policing seems to be widely acknowledged, however, there does not seem to be any appreciable impact in administration despite such knowledge. In general, much of the organizational control apparatus for law enforcement agencies is mired in the earlier forms of command

and control, quasi-military training, line and staff models of supervision, and rigid structures of rules and regulations. Such control mechanisms, an outgrowth of the Taylor model, have been around for most of the 20th century. In fact, some scholars argue that such controls have had tragic, unanticipated consequences for law enforcement organizations. Kelling provides another example as the bitter anti-management culture that is representative in many police departments to this day. Such a culture represents a "stay out of trouble" (de-policing) attitude that alienates officers from the community (p. 7).

In 1980, Lawrence Sherman reviewed two decades of quantitative research examining the causes of police behavior in the United States. In the early nineties, Riksheim and Chermak (1993) did a comparative analysis of Sherman's studies against research completed in the 1980s in similar areas of police behavior, which included the arrest variable. They found that whereas individual and situational characteristics were present, organizational factors were not even considered in the arrest process for the pre-1980s studies. In fact, organizational indicators received the least amount of quantitative attention during the 1980s research, despite the fact that they appeared to be consistent predictors of police behavior (p. 377). Riksheim and Chermak point out that studies examining organizational factors suggest significant variation among police agencies across the United States. In addition, explicit attempts to test theoretically derived propositions or hypotheses appeared uncommon, and theoretical explanations of quantitative findings were even less frequent in the studies.

Current theory has been inadequate in elucidating the phenomena of police discretion with respect to the organization, especially in informed explanations or propositions on how to guide such discretion. This is a significant problem since the prevailing view is that organizational factors are those over which police agencies have the most direct control. The challenge comes with reference to indoctrinating line officers as to the differences of proper discretion and "unnecessary," or improper discretion. Ironically, practitioners have used the term "common sense" to illustrate much of the discretionary behavior needed for police work; however, such a vague and ambiguous expression is inadequate for the true complexities involving such professional judgment.

Kenneth Culp Davis (1975), in his book *Police Discretion*, illustrated the need for administrative rulemaking in restricting the discretionary behavior of police. Nonetheless, even Davis lamented the need for great discretion on the part of police officers in conducting such a human service activity. But Davis was concerned with the problem of accountability and the fact that officers generally work alone, mostly free from direct observation of their supervisors.

Much of the research into police misconduct has used the individual as the unit of analysis. A new focus is emerging in which the examination is directed toward the police organization (Cannon, 1997). As early as the Wickersham Commission (1931), and more recently with the Christopher Commission (1991) and Rampart Area Corruption Investigation (2000), officials have been looking at the breakdown or lack of accountability mechanisms that lead to organizational dysfunction (Davis, 1975; Kelling, 1999; Walker, 2001).

Police administrators are beginning to realize that putting officers on the streets in a timely and organized fashion and getting them to particular locations rapidly is quite different from shaping police behavior once officers are out in the community dealing with citizens' problems, needs, and conflicts. Even Davis (1975), a strong proponent of "administrative rule-making," quickly acknowledged the need for discretion at the line level if the criminal justice system was to have any hope of operating effectively. Yet, Kelling (1999) warns that such empowerment begs questions from inside and outside the organization if we are to understand the delicate balance of discretionary decision-making and accountability. "What is the proper balance between individual rights and community interests? What do community collaboration, cooperation, and accountability really mean in an operational sense? How are police kept from protecting narrow parochial interests – such as keeping 'strangers' out of neighborhoods and communities? How do police refrain from doing what citizens should do for themselves or from usurping the roles of private or other governmental agencies?" (p. 12).

The exercise of discretion is not a simple matter. In most cases, the officer chooses one of several possible alternatives. Thus, controlling discretion is usually not a matter of simply forbidding something; it is more often a matter of encouraging officers to choose one option over another. Added to this, the arrest decision is extremely complex and can have significantly dangerous consequences for the officer, the suspect, and the organization. Consider a study of felony arrests done by Petersilia, Abrahamse, and Wilson (1987), that found that supervisors had little interest in the "quality" of arrests measured in terms of their ultimate outcomes. This is a disturbing declaration when associated with the allegation that most arrests do not result in formal criminal prosecution, much less conviction (Walker, 1993).

While there has been considerable research focus placed on individual, situational, and even community level indicators regarding police discretionary behavior, little has been done in the area of organizational effects. A review of the literature strongly suggests that such organizational indicators can have a significant impact on influencing such areas as police use of force (Skolnick and Fyfe, 1993). However, the effect of organizational variables on police arrest behavior seems to be unresolved (Riksheim and Chermak, 1993).

The concept of police discretion itself is relatively new, with many scholars pointing to the American Bar Foundation (ABF) study of the mid 1950s as the premier "discovery" event that changed the ministerial paradigm of policing, to one that recognized the existence of discretionary decision-making (Davis, 1975). Up to this point, many police administrators refused to even acknowledge that discretion played a part in policing.

The past two decades have seen growing awareness of the complexity of police work and an examination of the use of discretion in officers' daily policing activities. While the routine nature of police work tends to obscure the complexities involved with police discretion, few would argue that such decision-making is inconsequential. In fact, the point that a police officer's duties compel him to exercise personal discretion many times throughout a day is clearly evident, sometimes with catastrophic results. In a society that places tremendous value in personal liberty, the management of discretion by police officers can become a critical and difficult exercise.

Shaping the Decision-Making Process

The structure of hierarchy has been an important component to the discipline of police agencies throughout this country's history. Decisions not normally covered in policy manuals must often be evaluated by those higher in rank within the organization. Decision-making by street-level bureaucrats has typically been surrounded with a broad range of checks and balances.

Whether police work is a craft or a profession, it relies heavily upon experience and intuition. Such experience may rely on such superficial and ambiguous indicators as: appearance, stereotypes, ingrained organizational biases, and the like. This invariably has its hazards. A patrol officer can never completely rely upon the legitimacy of his authority to obtain compliance; citizens can and will resist even the most innocuous of requests. A street cop cannot resort to an arrest every time someone questions his authority, though there are clearly those who believe they can. Patrol officers are thus confronted with the necessity of developing and relying upon crude but sometimes effective strategies to gain compliance.

Many administrators refer to police agencies as quasi-military organizations with rigid organizational structures. This analogy is misleading, in part, because it fails to adequately describe the actual structure of a police department, and because such structures (military) are not suited to the requirements of the police task. Consider that the police function is normally carried out by officers working alone or in pairs, and only rarely are they forced into situations that require that they function as an organized unit – for example crowd control or planned events. Even specialization, a characteristic of professional police departments, has had little impact on the structure of such organizations. Investigative units such as detectives, vice squads, and traffic and juvenile bureaus have been organized to handle specialized problems, but the bulk of police activity is still the result of the decisions and actions of patrol officers. The patrol division of any police department operates as a more or less autonomous subsystem within the police bureaucracy, with communications routed directly to patrol officers.

What appears to bring the "quasi-military" feature to the surface is the emphasis on command and control. This has been a facet of the law enforcement structure since the inception of the first police agencies in this country. Unfortunately, control has come to denote a bureaucracy of punishment. One of the reasons the military was turned to as a model for the police was that it appeared to provide for a system of control and discipline that would eliminate the most egregious abuses of authority and misbehavior of the men and women engaged in police work (Rubinstein, 1973).

The prominence of obedience-based programs in law enforcement is further emphasized in its formal training programs. Some scholars argue that a good portion of training programs are superficially designed to acquaint rookies with the criminal law and department rules, and to develop a level of competency in certain proficiency skills (e.g., firearms), but the more important focus is to adjust the recruit to the disciplinary culture of the organization. Arthur Neiderhoffer (1976), a police officer turned scholar, has argued that the defining characteristic of recruit training is that it is a total and inclusive process which seeks to strip away the recruit's previous identity and values and replace them with those appropriate to the police role.

Critics argue that the "para-military" attitude of law enforcement executives illustrates their over-zealous proclivity for discipline; in part to demonstrate that they have control over the organization. However, reality lies closer to the difficulties of closely supervising police officers who work alone and the inability of such executives to specify, through policy guidelines, how a patrol officer should behave in various kinds of situations. Most of the formal administrative controls within a police department have very little to do with discretion. Hierarchichal controls set only the outer limits to the use of police power, while the day-to-day process of decision-making is played out free of restraint. The question is, why?

One reason may involve one of the strongest cultural norms in policing, that of "second-guessing" another officer. This principle maintains that the officer on the scene is in the best possible position, and is the most knowledgeable of the circumstances to make the decision. The supervisor who attempts to closely monitor the actions of his subordinates and fails to keep his distance will surely suffer the label of being a "micro-manager," and will be considered a hindrance to good police work.

Second, patrol officers are able to acquire considerable power within a police department, and this reinforces the normative limits to hierarchical controls while further limiting the ability of administrators to control the decisions of patrol officers. Police administrators and supervisors are caught between demand for loyalty to the men and women on the street and demands from the public that police power be used in a specific way or even curtailed. This dilemma is at the heart of a supervisor's relationship to the men and women under him.

Professional police agencies appear to be a creation of two distinct systems that have created a bifurcated arrangement of internal control. On the one hand, there is the bureaucratic conformity to rules, no matter how trivial, to demonstrate the success in police reform. On the other is the police culture, based on the regulation of behavior through the adherence to group norms, which idealizes individualism. The combination of these two systems adds to the conflict of contradictory objectives in the police task and the chaos in attempting effective control of police discretion.

Theoretical Framework for the Analysis of Administrative Discretion

Brown (1988) argues that the exercise of discretion by administrators and street-level bureaucrats is to be understood in terms of the way in which the structural characteristics of bureaucracies influence the implementation of public policy. Discretionary choices can be significantly impacted by the pressures and enticements generated by structural controls. Street-level bureaucrats will find ways to adapt to these pressures, which ultimately affect the way public policy is implemented. These pressures may be subtle routine practices, or more formalized use of organizationally derived decision rules to guide the implementation of policy.

The beginning of wisdom in the analysis of the implementation of public policy lies in realizing that many decisions are a response not to the nature of the clientele, the demands of interest groups, or even the intent of policy, but rather to internally generated bureaucratic pressures. This applies most forcibly to street-level bureaucrats in general, and to the police in particular.

Policy decisions are seldom self-implementing. Administrators are the ones that actually have to get their hands dirty and put decisions into effect. In applying this to street-level bureaucrats, such as the police, requires a clarification between the differences of discretion and policymaking. Using Brown's description of policymaking, it "is the act of choosing the norms – framing a law for example – to guide future actions, and necessarily involves unusual or non-routine choices." Brown goes on to explain that administrative discretion, by contrast, "is the act of making choices in light of policy norms, and involves routine but adaptive choices" (p. 25).

In the act of discretion, although the decision maker accepts a framework of values and goals, some aspects of the decision process are unspecified or contingent on circumstances and thus up to the judgment of the individual. To clarify the distinction between policymaking and discretion, Brown uses the example of a steersman on a ship. The decision of what course a ship will take between two points is a policy decision; but the decisions made by the steersman to maintain course while taking account of weather conditions and the like are discretionary decisions. More broadly, administrative discretion may be defined as the regulation of social and political processes in light of institutionalized political (legal) norms. No statute no matter how detailed, no rule book no matter how thick can anticipate all contingencies and program all administrative actions.

Discretion is structured by the decision-maker's belief system, and such choices will be based on their interpreted objectives of the policy mandate and their own objectives, interests, and needs. That decision-maker will view situations in light of prior values, making comparison of similar situations, and use a pre-defined set of alternatives to take actions that fundamentally shape the character and direction of public policy. No matter how chaotic, how unique a set of circumstances they encounter, decision makers approach them on the basis of learned responses to reasonably similar situations. As a result, a discrete set of values and facts are woven together and form a perceptual net that guides individual decisions. These perceptual nets, while representing belief systems, can be referred to as operational styles of an administrator (Brown, 1988; Wilson, 1968).

An operational style is an important determinant of the way an administrator or police officer will respond to events and is an important variable in explaining discretionary choices. Operational styles can be shaped by organizations and administrators control the choices of subordinates by influencing their beliefs. Whatever the dictates of an operational style might suggest in a given situation, an administrator or street-level bureaucrat is not entirely free to act in any way he chooses. The degree of autonomy an administrator possesses clearly varies. The freedom of action enjoyed by the police, for example, is far greater than that possessed by municipal librarians. The nature of the limits (or lack of limits) on an administrator's autonomy depends upon the factors that affect the latitude of administrative discretion.

Brown discusses two types of constraints that intrude upon the exercise of discretion: *environmental* and *organizational*. The environmental constraints are those exogenous forces that limit administrative autonomy or force consideration prior to implementing a policy. For street-level bureaucrats, this also includes the characteristics of their work environment: the objective characteristics and demeanor of clients, the adequacy of organizational resources, and broader characteristics of the community such as cultural traditions. The salience and impact of these environmental constraints often depend on more deeply rooted social and economic phenomena such as the rate of social and economic change, and the level of class or group conflict. Samples of these exogenous actors have been discussed in the section on *Influences on Governance.*

Organizational constraints refer to the system of administrative rules, policies, and managerial controls designed to ensure conformity to administrative directives. These include organizational structure (degree of centralization, division of labor); types of organizational controls (rules, incentives, recruitment and training procedures); and the behavior of administrators and supervisors. The impact of organizational constraints depends on the ability (and often the desire) of administrators to rationalize organizational processes, to bring under administrative control the decisions and behavior of subordinates.

It is important to note that there are differences between organizational elites and street-level bureaucrats when it comes to discretionary choices. The street police officer is enmeshed in a system of rules designed to govern their behavior, and subject to the watchful eye of supervisors and a host of training and indoctrination programs predicated on ensuring conformity in beliefs and values among organizational members. While organizational elites are responsible for mediating between the agency and the broader political and social environment, street-level bureaucrats have to manage environmental uncertainties directly with clients that confront the agency in the implementation of a policy or program. This limits the impact of administrative controls on street-level bureaucrats, but it does not afford the kind of autonomy that an organizational elite possesses. There is a paradoxical quality to a street-level bureaucrat's relationship to an administrative organization, for he is both autonomous and controlled. This paradox is the root of many conflicts and moral dilemmas faced by street-level bureaucrats.

The discretionary choices of street-level bureaucrats are largely shaped by the values and beliefs of the decision maker and the goals, incentives, and pressures of the bureaucracy. The decision rules, values, and priorities of operational discretionary choices are determined by the joint impact of the bureaucratic requirements for stability and the maintenance of integrity, and by the need for street-level bureaucrats to adapt to these organizational pressures while performing an arduous and difficult task. The interesting question in the analysis of administrative discretion is to understand the conditions under which a decision maker must or will conform to organizational constraints. The assumption is rather one of the continuing possibility of conflict between the values and beliefs of the street-level bureaucrat and the organization. The discretionary powers of street-level bureaucrats can be controlled to the degree that a public agency structures belief systems relevant to the task and narrows the latitude of discretion. The ability of city administrators to shape the belief systems of individual street-level bureaucrats and the degree of administrative control over specific decisions depend also on the ability of an organization to control environmental and task-related uncertainty. These uncertainties arise from the conflict generated between policy mandates and organizational goals. Agencies, like the police, faced with the demand for satisfactory solutions to intractable social problems, face immense difficulties in rationalizing organizational decision-making. Consequently, the latitude of discretion is rather broad and the criteria used to judge different events may be a manifestation of the personal values of the decision maker as much as the priorities and expectations of administrators.

The point of this analysis is very simple: Administrators, be they organizational elites or street-level bureaucrats, are key actors in American government. Directly and indirectly, formally and informally, they make decisions and take actions that fundamentally shape the character and direction of public policy. The implication is a responsibility to see that administrative discretion is applied as competently and responsibly as possible.

Police Accountability

There has been little tradition for systematic, official inquiry into governmental practice in this country. Where there has been inquiry into police practice it has commonly been precipitated by crisis, has been directed toward finding incompetence or corruption, and, whatever the specific finding, has failed to give attention to the basic law enforcement issues involved.

As early as 1967, the President's Commission on Law Enforcement and Administration of Justice was raising the concern over the appropriate methods for safeguarding the exercise of discretionary power by governmental agencies where judicial review was not feasible nor desirable. Because there is no "best" answer to the question of control over the exercise of discretionary power, it seems obviously desirable to encourage a multifaceted approach, stressing innovation and experimentation, with the hope that, in the process, enough will one day be learned to afford an adequate basis for deciding what methods are best.

One issue that seems overtly apparent, but risks some oversimplification in the interpretation, is the need to give police policymaking greater visibility. The complexities of policing along with its problems and solutions must be shared with the community. It requires methods of involving members of the community in discussion of the propriety of the policies; and developing in police a willingness to see this process as inherent in a democratic society and as an appropriate way of developing policies which are both effective and supported by the community (Goldstein, 1986).

Asserting appropriate controls over police practice requires the participation of an informed and articulate community that will be intolerant of improper police practice. A difficulty in the law enforcement field is that the groups that receive the most police attention are largely inarticulate, and these groups fail to utilize a formal system for the expression of views. There is need, therefore, for development within the minority community of the capacity and willingness to communicate views and dissatisfactions to the police (Skolnick & Fyfe, 1993).

The complexities of citizen demands on law enforcement agencies are only part of the overall problem. Other impediments to effective policing result from the organization itself. Many problems that exist in police work are organizational in nature and must be solved internally before police agencies can effectively undertake the problems of community service. Examples include: integration of the community policing philosophy; the arrest decision by police and the policies that drive such mechanisms; standards of accountability and value systems; and the difficulties in educating the public in the procedure of policing represent significant organizational issues that call for widespread change.

Most police executives are aware of the strategic planning process for establishing vision, values, mission, and goals, but many neglect their implementation strategies. Moving too fast or too slowly can have disastrous results. DeParis warns that while significant organizational change may be required, maintaining a suitable rate of change is essential because change can produce either organizational health or illness (2000, p. 108). Research into complexity theory[3] suggests that every system has an optimal rate of change, and that even within systems the optimal rate of change may vary (Byrne, 1999). Change in police departments should be introduced gradually, and then accelerated.

Community Policing

When reviewed from an analytical perspective the goals, "to serve and protect," become blurred the closer one scrutinizes the operation of law enforcement agencies. There are differing management philosophies and practices among the 18,000 police agencies in this country. There are problems in some communities that do not exist in some others. There are variations in the skill and commitment of police officers who, in actuality, reflect the type of community they police. In essence, the same words, "to serve and protect," might be on many police departments' patrol cars, but interpretation is left wide open to the many analysts engaged in the field.

Traditionally, police officers have been viewed as soldiers engaged in a war on crime. This view has had the detrimental effect of focusing on ineffective strategies for crime control while resulting in a major cause of police violence and civil rights violations. The "war model" inaccurately portrays a search and destroy mentality to banish crime, disorder, and the scourge of drugs (Skolnick and Fyfe, 1993). According to DeParis (2000) it does not help that many police departments continue to use a bureaucratic, closed-system approach in an ever-changing and intrusive external environment. Such an environment results in an unstable situation (p. 108).

Nevertheless, noteworthy changes in the policing philosophy have resulted in the movement towards community policing. Many feel that this movement is the result of police that have not been accountable to the community, but have served status quo interests. Researchers declare that the conversion from traditional policing to a community-

---

[3] Theory based upon chaos theory that evolution occurs most effectively through interaction.

oriented approach will be one of the most significant challenges affecting police organizations today (DeParis, 2000; Goldstein, 1990).

With the help of responsible citizens and progressive police administrators there have been tremendous accomplishments in developing a form of policing that better meets the needs of the community. But Goldstein (2000) complains that the term "community policing" tends to be used indiscriminately to encompass the most ambitious project in policing to the most mundane, without regard for its true meaning. Politicians, administrators and police executives exacerbate the problem by misleading citizens into expectations that community policing will provide instant solutions not only for the problems of crime, disorder, and racial tension but for many of the other acute problems that plague the community as well. Of course, the failure of superficial programs with the community-policing label then adds to the frustration of not only the community, but also the police officers involved.

One reaction in the law enforcement community has been to attempt definition and simplification of the community policing model. This presents a problem for such a complex process as policing. In fact, Goldstein argues, the field already suffers because so much in policing is oversimplified (p. 72).

The criminal justice system has traditionally categorized and defined crime, violence, and disorder into simple convenient terms that act to disguise amorphous, complex problems. Oversimplification places a heavy burden on the police and complicates the police task. Goldstein explains that the police respond with such equally simplistic terms as "enforcement" and "patrol" in which the community is familiar but does not understand the methods they embrace or their value. Goldstein is concerned that if community policing is used as just another generic response or simplistic characterization of the police function this truly innovative approach will quickly lose credibility (p. 72).

Another concern for police executives making the transition to community policing involves police accountability. As law enforcement looked for ways to develop closer ties to the community in terms of accountability, the two most common forms took the shape of community relations units and civilian review boards. As was previously discussed, the problem with civilian review boards was the focus primarily on the performance of individual officers, particularly on mistakes and incompetence, and not organizational issues. Community relations units, unfortunately, were destined for failure not having sufficient resources to carry the message to the community or being responsive to the community needs in terms of problem definition and solutions.

Community policing brings an advantage that the other two forms do not present. While civilian review boards concentrate on perceived or real abuses by the police, community policing focuses on the substantive issues of problems, crime, and quality of life in neighborhoods (Kelling et al., 2000). Kelling points out that in this way, both citizens and police bring certain insights to the table:

> Citizens bring to the relationship their sense of community, knowledge about the problems in their neighborhoods, their own capacities to solve problems, and the potential to support or authorize police action. Police bring to communities concerns not only for their welfare but for the constitutional rights and the welfare of all individuals and the community-at-large – thus, countervailing the tendencies of the neighborhood residents to be overly parochial or opposed to the legitimate interests of strangers or particular subgroups (p.274).

This type of accountability is unlike the conventional means used by police in the past. It requires an understanding with communities in a different relationship that can take several forms. Kelling et al. explain that one such form is the policy-setting procedure. Chief Robert Igleburger of Dayton, Ohio pioneered this practice during the 1960s. Having the community participate in the policy process will go a long way to reduce the unrealistic expectations and demands that citizens have of the police. Another form involves both police and citizens identifying what problems the police will deal with, the types of tactics that will be utilized, and the desired outcomes.

This understanding between both parties establishes mutual accountability and provides measures to evaluate performance. The police are still responsible to provide their professional knowledge, skills, and values. Likewise, it does not free citizens from their responsibility for their own safety.

Traditional policing in the form of command and control may have created the illusion of control, but often has done little more than that. These mechanisms of control have hindered the promotion of creativity and innovation by police officers. The belief is that community policing will not threaten police accountability, but that the proper management of community policing will add additional opportunities for the maintenance of accountability in police organizations (Kelling et al., 2000, p. 279).

Community oriented policing has become widespread, prevalent, and fashionable not because it has been proven to work, but because the alternatives to it have been proven to fail. Though there are differences in police practices, it is not clear how they affect the management of order, the enforcement of laws, or the maintenance of good community relations (Wilson, 1968). It seems clear that there is much to be gained in terms of police-community relations with the philosophy of community policing. However, difficulties in clarification of the concept and how it will ultimately affect police policy and accountability will require more time and research.

Finally, in addition to organizational change comes the prospect of societal change. Reiss (1985) believes that a core issue for today's police executive will be that of social change. Given the accelerating rate of societal change, law enforcement organizations will have to respond and possibly even work to shape such change. Reiss asks the question, "Can they (police executives) actively plan for changes in society and participate in planning the future of society, as well as responding to what takes place?" (p. 65). It is no longer acceptable, or an excuse, for administrators to take a reactionary posture. The police leader of today must take a hard dynamic view, one in which the organization helps shape the environment as well as respond to it. There are many in the professional policing field that believe the organization can direct their own future, not just be a victim to their environment.

Organizational Factors

While there has been considerable research focus placed on individual, situational, and even community level indicators regarding police discretionary behavior, little has been done in the area of organizational effects. The concept of police discretion is relatively new and raises diverging opinions in the application of how such behavior should be controlled. Current theory has been inadequate in elucidating the phenomena of police discretion with respect to the organization, especially in informed explanations or propositions on how to guide such discretion. This is a significant problem since the prevailing view is that organizational factors are those over which police agencies have the most direct control. The literature review in this chapter strongly suggests that organizational indicators can have an impact on influencing such areas as police discretion, especially in the arrest decision process.

In sum, the arrest decision represents a major gap when placed in the conceptual area of discretion control. There is no reason not to begin to think about those factors that impact the critical arrest decision, especially in the area of the organizational level of scrutiny, which has been gravely lacking. This study explores such phenomena in the hopes of leading to a better understanding of such objects.

CHAPTER 3

Measuring Organizational Influence

This section identifies the research methodology and data collection techniques that are used for this study of organizational influence on police officer arrest discretion. Hence the objective is to elaborate on the step-by-step sequence of actions—or research design—that is used in this investigation. Such design is essential to obtaining meaningful and reliable information. While the main thrust of this research is exploratory, it was anticipated that analysis would provide components of description and explanation. The chapter addresses research issues in five sections: measuring arrest discretion, correlates of arrest discretion, review of research questions, data collection procedures and data analysis plan.

A comparatively small number of arrests in this country results in any appreciable prosecution, and an even smaller number results in conviction. However, police agencies maintain that one of their primary objectives is supporting the prosecution of criminals. Critics argue that such a formal position of action is utilized to maintain a level of lawful justifiability and to display quantitative evidence as to the effectiveness of the organization. The police can maintain that they have done their job, and the breakdown of the system comes from the failure of prosecutors to prosecute, or the reluctance of courts to keep criminals confined.

The police are well aware of the small percentage of arrests that are selected for prosecution. Indeed, this tends to confirm the use of arrest as a front-end intervention. Such practices, with little real intent for prosecution, make both the citizenry and the police vulnerable. However, most law enforcement administrators, when confronted with the issue, would maintain that the powers of arrest should not be used in a discriminating manner. Nevertheless, the discriminate use of arrest can become perfunctory and any control or review over the quality of arrests made by the police becomes inoperative. Without such review, programs in which arrest has been used as an end in itself tend to degenerate; they lead to sloppy practices in which individuals are taken into custody without adequate evidence. When this occurs, arrest becomes a program of summary punishment invoked by the police for violating whatever standards or rules they establish.

One way to achieve some level of control over the use of arrests is for the organization to establish effective management over the arrest procedure followed by officers. That is, the organization establishes both formal norms (rules) and informal norms regarding arrests that insure that due process is ingrained, that an adequate basis for each arrest exists, and that fairness and equality are appropriately considered. These features then can shape arrest behavior at the street-level decision point (individual police officers). For the purposes of this study, it is assumed that street-level discretion by field officers can be affected by organizational procedures and norms.

Conceptually, organizational influence on police officer discretion is multi-faceted. That is, different aspects of organizational characteristics and processes combine to create a particular level of organizational constraint or influence on officer arrest discretion. Davis (1975) discusses this concept in terms of values that range from complete control of discretion (no individual leeway) to unfettered discretion (no constraints on officer decisions). At one end of the scale, options are minimal, or non-existent in some cases, since a rule governs. At the other end of this spectrum is "unfettered discretion," which includes the decision to do nothing. Davis is careful to point out that this does not mean there is a point at which the law ends and discretion begins. This thinking supplements Wilson's (1968) cross-classifications of police departments, whereby we can infer that constraints will vary (as below) by the nature of the department. Thus, departments seen as militaristic tend to attempt the highest levels of control through an extensive and rigid rule structure. Consequently, these departments offer little officer discretion. This level of control gradually declines as one moves across the scale through legalistic, service and fraternal police departments. It is in the fraternal departments that one would expect to see the lowest levels of attempted control, resulting in the highest levels of officer discretion (see Figure 3).

Military	Legalistic	Service	Fraternal
----- -------------------	--------------------	--------------------	-----
Very Rigid Rule		Unfettered Discretion	
(Strong Department Control)		(Little Control)	

Figure 3. Organizational styles and their influence on discretion.

The measurement process is a deductive exercise in which one clarifies and specifies the meaning of concepts (abstractions) while identifying appropriate variables (indicators) for study. In this case, the concept of interest is the department's influence on police discretion, and the unit of analysis is the police department. The importance of the arrest decision in the field (patrol), and how the organization influences such discretion provides the focus for this research. Thus, conceptual interest is in defining discretion in arrest decisions that flows from structural, procedural, and attitudinal features of a department. The research literature indicates that the way an organization creates a structure for arrest discretion flows from four principal sources: official policy, process, training, and values. These dimensions capture the channels through which organizational management can attempt to influence or constrain the arrest behavior of officers.

In measuring organizational influence over police discretion, it is necessary to isolate the structural, process, and attitudinal characteristics. The dimensions of meaning referred to previously help to capture and conceptualize the element of meaning in police discretion. The dimensions described hereafter have been used for constructing a scale to measure capacity for organizational influence (control) of police discretion, herein referred to as the Arrest Discretion Control Scale (ADCS). In all, four dimensions of organizational constraint on arrest behavior are considered and include: policy, process, training, and values. It is crucial to remember that the issue in measurement of organizational constraints on officer discretion is *not the absolute amount of discretion* that is permitted. Instead, the focus is upon the extent to which the organization attempts to control the exercise of discretion, where discretion is characterized as the ability of the officer to deviate from department procedures and norms.

There is a *policy dimension* associated with every organization and it is particularly important among social control agencies. Policy has long been considered one of the most effective methods in guiding professional police judgment. Davis (1975) originally argued that administrative rulemaking should govern every police action. While Davis has modified his views in this area, it is important to point out that most police agencies rely heavily on rules and procedures to successfully perform their mission. The literature suggests that the more extensive and detailed policies are within the organization, the more control over discretionary decision-making.

In the deductive process of measurement, the challenge with specifying conceptual dimensions is that they must—to be studied—be converted to concrete elements (variables or indicators) that are meaningful in the world of experience (Kaplan, 1964). Conceptually, each indicator needs to be different from other indicators in that each measures a different aspect of the specified dimension. This is consistent with the statistical notion that indicators should be additive, such that the accumulation of the indicators individually capture different aspects of the dimension and collectively they represent the conceptual space defined by the dimension (Blalock, 1982). In this research, five aspects of the degree to which the organization, *through policy*, attempts to influence arrest behavior of officers are adopted.

The first of the concrete indicators measures the *specificity* of written arrest policy. The aim is to determine the presence of four particular elements of the written arrest policy: namely the presence of intent, authority, seizure and understanding. While numerous attempts have been made to frame an all-inclusive definition of arrest, this becomes a difficult task because the term has so many applicable situations. However, the courts have set out basic elements that are necessary to constitute an arrest. These elements are:

1. A purpose or intention to effect an arrest of a person;
2. The authority, by law or statute, to make the arrest, and in most cases communication by the arresting officer to the one whose arrest is sought of such intent and purpose.
3. An actual or constructive seizure or detention of the person to be arrested by one having the present power to control him;

4. An understanding by the person who is to be arrested that it is the intention of the arresting officer then and there to arrest and detain such person.

Clearly written guidelines described in operations manuals covering these elements of arrest establish a foundation for valid arrests and the rights guaranteed by the Fourth Amendment to the Constitution. In terms of organizational attempts to control discretion, specific written procedures indicate that the department is attempting to constrain officer decisions and make sure that such decisions conform to department policy.

The second concrete indicator focuses upon the department's use of professional legal review of written arrest procedures. Such reviews are important in that it formalizes the policy process for developing guidelines that set standards, shape the inevitable use of discretion, and support involvement by legal and administrative partners of the judicial system. Consequently, the presence of such review of arrest procedures indicates that the department can influence (increase) control over the proper exercise of police discretion in the decision making process.

A third indicator of policy-based constraints can be captured as the organization's attempt to direct necessary discretion in the arrest decision process. Police departments should develop and enunciate policies that give police personnel specific guidance for the common situations requiring the exercise of police discretion. This includes such matters as the handling of minor disputes, the issuance of orders to citizens regarding their movements or activities, and the decision of whether or not to arrest in specific situations involving specific crimes.

Still another indicator of policy constraints on arrest behavior can be found in the presence of external review procedures in the policy process. This differs from administrative review in that it involves multiple partners external to the organization (citizen panels, town halls, businesses, politicians, etc.). The police should prepare proposed rules on the basis of staff studies (as stated earlier), publish them, invite written comments from members of the community and the organization, make feasible revisions on the basis of the comments, and then publish the final rules. Such reviews will help to screen out deficient, out-dated directives and to insure *uniformity* across officers in arrests. The basic goal is preventive: to identify problems or potential problems and to correct them before they result in a major crisis such as a questionable shooting, a lawsuit, or a serious disturbance. Subsequently, it is hypothesized that such reviews provide enhanced control for the organization over police discretion in determining whether and when to enforce particular law.

Finally, the fifth indicator of interest here is the *extensiveness* of departmental arrest policy. That is, does department policy attempt to devise a rule for every possible arrest situation? Almost certainly, patrol officers would be better off if they had a clearer idea of what administrators expect of them in different situations. More explicit policies would reduce some of the uncertainties patrol officers face. However, just as there are limits to specifying all contingencies when devising a law, so there are limits to the ability of police administrators to devise rules which will cover the wide variety of situations patrol officers encounter. While there is a need for the police to more consciously make policy, devising a rule for every situation is no substitute for the development of judgment. In particular, are officers allowed to consider time, location, condition of offender, conditions of the victim or witness, and volume or frequency of the offense in determining whether to make an arrest? It is hypothesized that as extensiveness increases in arrest policy there is a corresponding decrease in officer discretion, making this an organizational constraint on discretion.

A second important dimension to the way that departments attempt to influence officer discretion in arrests can be found in the *process or procedural requirements* associated with making arrests. This process dimension involves organizational imposition of procedures that must be followed for officers to effect an arrest. The process dimension includes structural processes that are in place to enhance professional judgment, correct deficiencies, or serve as a warning device to potential problems in unwarranted discretion. Using such procedures allows the management of the organization to exercise influence over arrest decisions through procedurally required supervisory scrutiny and the imposition of sanctions for failures to comply.

Five indicators were chosen as important aspects of process or procedural requirements imposed by police departments. Three of these deal with different aspects of the level of supervisory scrutiny of officer arrest decisions. They are different (additive) in that they represent differing degrees of directness of intervention at different times in the arrest process. Furthermore, the presence of one level of intervention does not necessarily mean that other levels will automatically be present or absent in a given department's procedures. The first of these three indicators represents the earliest and most direct—face-to-face—intervention. Thus, this indicator determines if a supervisor is expected to review the circumstances at the scene and approve the arrest prior to booking. Some research has determined that the presence of police supervisors increases the likelihood of arrest (Smith and Klein, 1983; Smith, 1984). However, the relationship was confounded by department type. When a supervisor was present, arrest was more likely in militaristic and legalistic departments but less likely in fraternal departments. It is believed that the presence of a supervisor forces the officer to consider department rules and closer conformance to the letter of the law. Therefore, face-to-face intervention represents an organizational constraint on officer discretion. The second intervention represents a slightly more delayed intervention, taking place without the direct presence of the arresting officer. Thus, this indicator asks whether the department has a review process for all field arrests conducted by a supervisor or detective prior to the preliminary (probable cause) hearing. Within the structure of some police agencies this is referred to as a "case agent" who may review the appropriateness and legality of the arrest and corresponding criminal charges. While this *after-the-fact* review may not appear to constrain police discretion at the time, the organization has the ability to reprimand or counsel the officer for *bad* arrests, thereby, giving impact to future constraint on arrest discretion. Another benefit of this type of review is the opportunity for the agency to ask for dismissal of charges in a faulty arrest, thereby, limiting harm to the arrestee.

The third indicator attempts to capture the extent to which upper management communicates recurrent problems about arrest incidents to its employees. As stated earlier, *bad* arrests may be identified by a supervisor, a case agent, or even through a formal auditing process. This may take place long after the arrest with the information on the deficiencies placed into a database or tracking system for use in aggregate reviews. Communicating such recurrent problems to employees can significantly minimize or reduce future problems. While policies are generally formulated to deal with such issues, many officers complain that a policy takes too long to address the issue and that publishing repeated arrest deficiencies is much more effective and timely. Once more, this may not have an impact on the initial arrest, but the process acts as an organizational constraint to future arrest decisions. In addition, the presence of such communication provides notice to other officers that there is a review process on arrests, thus, providing an organizational constraint on arrest discretion. The fourth and fifth indicators of the process dimension measures the extent to which *discovery* of procedural violations exist, and the presence of formal *sanctions* imposed for officers deemed to have not complied with established procedures. As far back as the research on industrial bureaucracy by Alvin Gouldner (1954), it has been known that supervisors and managers have the ability to exercise "leeway" in the enforcement of existing procedures and rules. That is, rules and procedures may be present, but their differential enforcement can greatly reduce the extent to which employees, in this case officers, are actually constrained in their work-related behaviors. These two indicators differ in that one focuses upon the *discovery* of noncompliance, while the other addresses the *severity* of sanctions. In addressing discovery, department representatives are asked to respond to the claim that "this department has organizational mechanisms in place to detect all but very minor violations of arrest procedures." With respect to severity of punishment, department representatives are asked to judge the statement that "this department places strong emphasis on formal discipline for any officer that intentionally violates arrest procedures."

The third dimension of organizational influence on officer discretion addresses the issue of *training*. In all organizations, training represents the chief way in which policy and procedures are translated into behavior expectations for employees. Training also insures that employees have the elemental ability to execute the organizational expectations. In this study, the training dimension, as an avenue for making department expectations clear and operational, is examined in terms of *extensiveness, content,* and the *monitoring of effectiveness* of arrest procedure training.

With respect to extensiveness of training, concern in creating indicators focuses upon when an officer is trained regarding arrest procedures and levels of reinforcement that are provided for that training. There are three indicators of concern here. All officers receive some training on arrest procedures in the academy, yet it is known that the initial street experience may or may not influence this training. Hence, in this study, department representatives will be queried regarding the extent to which Field Training Officers emphasize the understanding of official arrest procedures during the new officer's initial experience on the street. The integration of academic and practical application is an important indicator of the organization's commitment to civil rights, proper arrest procedure, and *shaped* discretion when it comes to the arrest decision process. Legal advisors teaching in the academy may be very astute to criminal law and court procedure; however, many police officers can attest to their first day on the street and being told to forget what they learned in the academy, that they were going to learn how it is really done on the street. A second indicator is found in the *frequency* with which all officers are required to have training on departmental arrest procedures. This has the effect of emphasizing to experienced officers that department procedures must be followed regarding arrests. To capture this indicator, department representatives are asked to consider the statement, "patrol officers frequently receive formal refresher training in arrest procedures." Finally, the measures of extensiveness must also capture whether department training in arrest procedures is disseminated to supervisory levels. This approach to training emphasizes that, not just officers, but also supervisors must know and adhere to departmental arrest procedures.

The fourth indicator of the training dimension focuses explicitly on whether the content of training directly addresses the notion of officer discretion. This is an important issue because training that does not directly address discretion may create the impression that discretion is unregulated, or that an undefined amount of officer discretion is implicitly permitted. Determining whether department training directly defines the tolerance of and extensiveness of officer deviations from department policy in making arrests can be used to measure this indicator.

Finally, the fifth indicator of the training dimension addresses the extent to which the department monitors the effectiveness of training on arrest procedures. Departments that fall more toward the fraternal end of Wilson's classification system may have training for arrest procedures but may trust that procedures are functional without testing. Any department that does not measure the effectiveness of its arrest training risks the introduction of officer discretion (through interpretation) into arrest practices. Departments that are serious about managing officer discretion will not just engage in training, but will actively assess the effectiveness of that training and modify it to insure that the "correct" procedures are not only appropriately taught but in fact learned. To measure this indicator, it will be determined if departments operate a system to evaluate the effectiveness of arrest procedure training and use the evaluation information to enhance the effectiveness of the training.

The last dimension of the extent to which department's attempt to constrain arrest processes addresses the notion of departmental *values*. This dimension represents an attempt to capture the effects of police culture on the practice of arrests by officers. It is argued that the professional ethos of the organization sets the tone for its members. As police agencies work on developing relationships with the community, police executives need to find ways to guide discretion and police behavior generally through increasing reliance on values instead of relying strictly on rules and protocols of accountability. It is postulated that police agencies with high levels of discretionary control will incorporate a rigorous value system into their culture.

Measuring "police culture" is a difficult and challenging endeavor. In measuring the values dimension regarding arrest decisions, the intent is to capture a narrow construct: departmental norms regarding the individual responsibility and discretion regarding arrests. Five indicators of the values dimension are used in this study to measure perceptions of department values, including citizen participation and policing philosophy and perceptions of individual responsibility.

The first three indicators address the values notion in general by soliciting information about departmental norms regarding independence, professionalism, and the relationship of management to officers on the street. With respect to independence, concern is with the departmental norms or expectations regarding the latitude permitted individuals in carrying out their duties. Thus, one may operationalize this indicator by asking for a reaction to the claim that "it is acknowledged in this department that officers will sometimes make arrest decisions that are based on criteria not covered by written policy or standard procedure." To the extent that this norm of independence is respected, one would anticipate higher levels of tolerance of officer discretion. In addressing professionalism, the concern is with the congruence of officer behavior with departmental interpretations of the law. In departments where it is determined that this congruence must always be high, one would expect that a lower level of control over officer arrest discretion is practiced. To measure professionalism, one can determine the extent to which it is believed that "the police should always operate in an atmosphere that requires them to invoke impartially all criminal laws within the bounds of full enforcement." Measuring the environment of the department manager support of officer decisions is a means of soliciting information on how much leeway is permitted to officers in general. While this is a complex notion, one indicator that may be used is an assessment of the extent to which an officer making a mistake is treated as a discipline problem. To the extent that discipline is universally imposed, the department more closely resembles the militaristic end of Wilson's (1968) continuum, and consequently may be seen as providing an atmosphere that is not conducive to the exercise of discretion. One can measure this approach by asking whether "the department permits the use of discretion as an excuse for policy violations of arrest procedures."

Another aspect of the values dimension of department governance of arrest outcomes is the extent to which citizens are involved in reviews of arrests and arrest practices. The current popularity of community policing philosophies in law enforcement demands that citizens and their interests are considered in all aspects of department behavior and function. The extent of community interest incorporation can be measured through the use of two indicators. The first is direct and involves citizen participation. For this indicator, one must determine if the "department supports the use of a review board that includes citizens to conduct reviews of serious police misconduct involving arrests." Critics of professional police administration argue that after generations of reform-minded police executives have attempted to control police behavior that accountability is still a low-level priority in the police culture. The basic goal of citizen oversight is to open up the historically closed complaint process, to break down the self-protective isolation of the police, and to provide independent, citizen perspective on such complaints. Research on civilian review shows that participating members tend to be educated in department policies and procedures and that the main thrust of such review is whether there has been a policy violation. Thus, it is hypothesized that agencies that incorporate civilian review will have higher levels of discretionary control. The second indicator is focused more on the philosophy of arrest that prevails in the department relative to perceptions of community interest. In this case, one asks whether the "department promotes community-policing interests over considerations of individual rights in arrest situations." Community policing raises new issues related to accountability. To a great extent, it accentuates the problems associated with traditional police management, primarily by decentralizing responsibility within police departments and asking rank-and-file officers to exercise even greater discretion than in the past. Much of the progress in police accountability in recent decades has been achieved through centralized control over police officer discretion – through court imposed rules or internal rules and procedures. The literature on community policing has given relatively little attention to the fundamental tension between decentralized responsibility and centralized control in policing. In departments that do stress the concern with community interests, one would expect that the level of officer discretion tolerated is higher.

The preceding discussion has specified four dimensions of departmental attempts to constrain discretion, and for each dimension five specific indicators have been elaborated. Through these dimensions and indicators, the conceptual *meaning* of organizational influence on arrest discretion has been described. The twenty indicators capture the different aspects of organizational attempts to influence discretion that must be translated into research terms to effectively measure the concept. This presents the measurement challenge that multiple questions must be asked to determine the placement of any given department (the unit of analysis) relative to attempts to control discretion. Yet at the same time, one must somehow combine the answers to all twenty questions in a meaningful way to obtain a single, composite measure for analysis. Methodologically, this challenge is met through the use of a multi-item scale (Babbie, 1998). Generically, a scale permits the inclusion of multiple questions in the creation of a composite measure. Since the dimensions and indicators developed above were constructed to be additive, an appropriate scaling technique is that of Summated Ratings (Edwards, 1957; Henerson, Morris and Fitz-Gibbon, 1987). The first summated ratings scale was developed by Rensis Likert (Edwards, 1957), and these types of scales are often labeled "Likert scales". In developing a Likert scale, one first assembles the items to be scaled. The twenty items representing indicators of the four dimensions of "organizational influence on arrest discretion" are enumerated as follows.

1. Policy Dimension
    A. Specificity of arrest policy
    B. Professional legal review
    C. Shaped discretion (necessary)
    D. External review
    E. Extensiveness of arrest policy
2. Process/Procedure Dimension
    A. Face-to-face intervention
    B. Case agent review
    C. Communication
    D. Discovery of procedural violations
    E. Severity of sanctions
3. Training Dimension
    A. Comprehensiveness of field training
    B. Frequency of arrest procedure training
    C. Supervisory training
    D. Discretionary choices
    E. Monitoring effectiveness of training
4. Values Dimension
    A. Independence
    B. Professionalism
    C. Relationship of management
    D. Citizen review
    E. Community policing

Once the items are assembled, the cumulating aspect of the scale must be addressed. This process, for Likert scales, assumes that each scale item is a statement (either positive or negative) related to the concept of interest, that the statements are additive in nature, and that "subjects or respondents" will be asked to express their degree of agreement or disagreement with each item. It is by assigning numeric values to the response format (or answer choices) that one begins the process of scoring the scale. When Likert invented summated ratings scales, he used five answer choices, beginning with Strongly Agree (with the statement) and progressing through Strongly Disagree. These five choices are commonly still used with Likert scales, although as

Edwards (1957) points out, some authors choose to vary the choices in a variety of ways, including not using a "neutral" category and adding additional categories of agreement. For the purposes of this study, an alternative response format was employed that adds categories of agreement to Likert's original five. Thus, the following six categories are used as the response format in this study:

Table 1. Likert Scale Categories for Survey Instrument

Strongly Agree	Agree	Somewhat Agree	Somewhat Disagree	Disagree	Strongly Disagree

In most Likert-type scales there is a midpoint that usually carries the idea of neutrality – neither agree nor disagree, for example. A neutral category is not used in this study because, given the nature of police department approaches to arrests, it would not be meaningful. An even number of response choices forces informants to "take a stand," while an odd number of choices lets informants "sit on the fence." The ultimate scoring for a summated rating scale is very straightforward. The response choices for each item are assigned, as above, a numeric value ranging from 1 through 6. Some items are worded such that agreement with the item indicates that the department is attempting to control discretion. Since we want higher numeric values of the scale to reflect higher levels of attempted control of discretion, items that are structured in this way have a value of 6 assigned to strongly agree and each item choice after is numerically smaller until strongly disagree receives a value of 1. Some items are worded such that disagreement with the item represents a higher level of attempted control of discretion. These items have been reverse coded, such that strongly disagree is assigned a value of 6, with subsequent items receiving smaller values through strongly agree which is assigned a value of 1. There are no formal guidelines about the mix (or proportion) of positively worded versus negatively worded items in Likert scales (Likert, 1932). Finally, to obtain a scale score, the numeric value of the response to each item was summed and then divided by the number of items in the scale (in this case, twenty). This yields a scale with values ranging from 1.0 (very low level of departmental control of discretion) through 6.0 (very high level of departmental control of discretion).

The Arrest Discretion Control Scale (ADCS) was tested for reliability using a "test-retest" technique (Edwards, 1957). Twelve sworn officers from Phoenix and Tempe Police Departments were used as the group on which the scale was pre-tested. Each of the participants in this procedure was the rank of Commander or higher and understood police operations regarding arrest procedures. After the scale was administered, the order of presentation of items was randomized and the scale was re-administered to the same group nine days later. The time required for each person to complete the questionnaire was recorded and comments on each question were solicited. The times to complete the questionnaire ranged from six minutes to fifteen minutes with a median of eleven minutes. The Pearson's Product-moment correlation between the first administration and the second administration was $r^2 = .816$. Using Edwards (1957) criterion that correlations above .80 represent acceptable reliability, the Arrest Discretion Control Scale (ADCS) was judged to be reliable.

Correlates of Organizational Influence

In terms of the research questions presented initially in Chapter 1, there are two thrusts of this study. First, there is a concern with understanding the extent to which police departments attempt to control discretion. Departmental influence on discretion is measured using a Likert scale. By examining the different levels or scale scores that departments achieve on this measurement, one can begin to describe the prevalence of such control behaviors among a sample of police departments. Second, it is possible to identify other variables that, theoretically, should be correlated with departmental attempts to control discretion and test those relationships in the data set.

Numerous factors that constitute characteristics of the organization may be identified that can be expected to affect the dependant variable of organizational control of discretion in field arrests. The correlates studied here are measured at the organizational level of analysis (consistent with the dependent variable of organizational influence on arrest discretion) and represent structural characteristics of police departments that might be expected to be related to the dependent variable. After reviewing the literature on police department organization and discretion, four correlates were identified that are likely to be associated with department attempts to influence the exercise of discretion. Each of these correlates is examined in this section; both nominal and operational definitions are presented, and the logic for how each is related to attempted influence over discretion is elaborated. The four correlates are bureaucracy, professionalism, department size, and supervision.

Bureaucracy

The word "bureaucracy" has been used rather loosely in the police literature, but there does appear to be some consensus on the characteristics that bureaucratic police departments share. Bureaucratic police departments are thought to have a high degree of vertical differentiation (a tall rank structure), in which efficiency, discipline, and productivity are stressed (Bittner, 1970; Manning, 1997). This high degree towards the military model tends to stress regulations, hierarchy, and obedience (Skolnick, 1966). Officers learn to place high importance on following the rules to avoid punishment, and this rigid conception of order places emphasis on crime control behavior. For purposes of this study, bureaucracy is operationalized as the number of levels of management between the police chief and line-level officers, and the number of divisions within the department.

Professionalism

Professional police organizations have been characterized in many different ways making operationalization difficult. Such departments are thought to be agencies in which education, service, and citizen respect are central (Goldstein, 1977). Professional departments may have tall or shallow rank structure but generally have wide ranges of specialty units. Having specialty units (e.g., crime prevention unit, community relations, school resource officer, etc.) is believed to demonstrate a department's commitment to community service. In addition, professional police departments may be identified by various factors such as college incentive pay, community relations training, and percentage of officers who are college educated (Smith and Klein, 1983). For purposes of this study, a mix of Crank's (1990) and Goldstein's (1977) characterization of professionalism is operationalized as follows; 1) the amount of entry level education required for police officers, and 2) the number of specialty units within the department.

Department Size

While department size can be measured in a variety of ways, this study will focus on the number of sworn personnel in a department. Research is mixed on the impact of department size on discretionary decisions to arrest. Mastrofski, Ritti, and Hoffmaster (1987) found that officers in smaller departments were more likely to arrest than their larger department counterparts. The willingness of officers to arrest decreased as department size and level of bureaucracy increased. However, Brown (1988) found that officers in large departments experienced more latitude and autonomy and were more inclined to act (arrest). There is the presumption that large departments have less effective controls on their members, less group stability, and a weaker link to the community that tends to subtract from the service style of policing. This makes it difficult to describe whether the relationship of size will have a direct or inverse relationship with discretionary influence.

Supervision

This deals with the span of control for field (street) supervisors. One obvious way a supervisor has of influencing discretion and maintaining some control over patrol officers is simply by being present at the scene of a call. Those police departments that have a high number of officers for each supervisor are expected to have less effective controls on their members. Interestingly, some research found that the presence of police supervisors increased the likelihood of arrest. Smith and Klein (1983) found that militaristic and legalistic departments, especially, produced more arrests when an on-scene supervisor was present. Kelling argues that in today's litigious society, along with the risk of discipline involved in improper arrest procedures, that officers are more likely to avoid arrest situations if at all possible. Lack of supervision can enhance such avoidance.

For purposes of this study, supervision will be operationalized as the number of patrol officers normally assigned to one field supervisor, keeping in mind that many agencies have policy limits on span of control even though the actual numbers may fluctuate slightly.

Review of Research Questions

The purpose of this section is to briefly review the research questions for the study and to state expectations regarding the likely answer (or relationship that will be obtained in the data analysis) for each question.

What is the observed range of organizational influence on police officer discretion in field arrests among police departments as measured on the Arrest Discretion Control Scale (ADCS)? This Likert-type scale is used to identify the central tendency and dispersion of the departments studied with respect to their capacity for organizational influence over discretionary choices in the arrest decision process. The scale measures organizational influence over discretion from low (1.0 on the scale) to high (6.0 on the scale).

What is the relationship between organizational bureaucracy and the influence on police officer discretion in field arrests? As indicated previously, organizational bureaucracy will be measured by a couple of indicators that are interrelated (rank structure and divisions). It is believed that highly bureaucratic departments become focused on a "conception of order," meaning strict compliance with rules and regulations. Therefore, it is postulated that the higher the bureaucratic composition of a police department the more significant will be the organizational influence over discretionary decision making regarding field arrests.

What is the relationship between organizational professionalism and the influence on police officer discretion in field arrests? There are two aspects of organizational professionalism selected for exploration in this research which include (1) the amount of entry level education required for police officers to be a member of the department, and (2) the number of specialty units within the department. While past studies have produced varied and confusing results (Smith and Klein, 1983) regarding the effect of professionalism on the arrest decision process, commitment to education and the orientation to community service (specialized units) is expected to increase the flexibility of discretionary choices for police officers. It is hypothesized that the higher the level of professionalism for a department the lower the level of organizational control over discretionary arrest decisions.

How are organizational size and the degree of influence over police officer discretion in field arrests related? Department size can be measured in a variety of ways, however, for purposes of this research size will relate to the number of sworn (police officers) personnel in the department. It is postulated that the measures of size will be inversely correlated with organizational influence of police officer arrest discretion.

What is the relationship between supervisory span of control and the organizational influence on police officer discretion in field arrests? Those police departments that have a high ratio of officers to supervisor are expected to have less control of their members. Mastrofski (1981) argues that a large span of control provides less group stability, reduced oversight, and limited time that a supervisor can spend with an employee. It is anticipated that departments with a low ratio of officers to supervisor will have elevated influence over police discretionary choices in field arrests.

Data Collection Plan

The scope of this study is national, focusing on the population of all police departments in the United States with 200 or more sworn officers. Substantively, the focus is upon departmental attempts at control of arrest discretion, and with specifying the relationship of four correlates (characteristics of departments) with this dependent variable. The principal mechanism of data collection was a mailed questionnaire.

The population of this research is the 211 municipal police departments in the United States with 200 or more sworn officers. A list of police departments described in the population was obtained from the National Directory of Law Enforcement Administrators (1999), and a database was created to maintain the data. Since the total number of such departments is small, all were included in the study; thus, this research constitutes a census of departments rather than a sample. Since only departments with 200 or more sworn officers were used, any knowledge of smaller police departments is precluded from this study. This raises the issue of validity as to whether research results will apply to smaller agencies, non-municipal agencies, and those that reside outside the United States. The population for this study was restricted to such law enforcement agencies described above for practicality purposes. Since the focus of research is on the arrest decision process and discretion, the main thrust in the sampling frame was to expose those agencies with a more significant number of arrest incidents. Theoretically, it is believed that organizational structures and styles that influence control of discretion in median to large police departments will apply to smaller law enforcement agencies in the United States. While similar results may be found in police agencies in developed countries, it is unclear how such results would apply in undeveloped countries.

A short questionnaire that included measures of departmental influence on arrest discretion, each of the four correlates and other information was assembled (see Appendix A). The questionnaire was mailed to the police chief of each of the listed departments requesting that he or she complete the form, or that a command-level employee in charge of the patrol function complete the survey. These positions are considered to be the best source of information regarding department characteristics and knowledge regarding policy, procedures, training, and organizational values. While it is expected that some police departments delegated different respondents to answer particular questions (e.g., structural questions relating to size, divisions, education costs, and specialty details), each questionnaire asked for information on the primary person responsible for completing the instrument. Of the total surveys returned, the breakdown in rank structure of the respondents is as follows; chiefs of police (12.2%), assistant police chiefs (9.5%), middle managers such as captains, commanders, and majors (19%), lieutenants (15.6%), sergeants (20.4%), and non-sworn civilian personnel (8.8%).

Using Dillman's (1978) protocol, a standardized mailing was utilized to obtain research data. A cover letter explaining the purpose and sponsorship of the study was enclosed with each questionnaire, and each respondent had the opportunity to return the completed questionnaire by fax or in a pre-addressed, pre-paid mailing envelope. The original surveys were prepared on light green paper in an effort to increase the number of returns (Fox et al., 1988). After 14 days, a follow up electronic mailing (e-mail) and an additional copy of the questionnaire were sent to the departments that had not yet responded. For departments that did not answer either the mailed or electronic questionnaire, phone contact was made and the questions were asked in interview fashion. The process yielded a total of 147 completed questionnaires at the time analysis was conducted, from the total of 211 mailed surveys. The first mailing produced 123 returns, and the second electronic mailing yielded 23 additional returns. One completed phone interview was conducted.

Data Analysis

There are two analytical goals in this inquiry. The first is to characterize the extent to which police departments attempt to influence arrest discretion. The second is the more theoretical aim of examining the relationship of the four correlates described in this chapter with attempted influence over arrest discretion. To characterize prevalence, descriptive statistics have been used to document the central tendency and dispersion of departments along the Arrest Discretion Control Scale (ADCS). Simple correlational analysis was utilized to describe the relationships among the four conceptual dimensions that compose the scale.

The second goal of this research rests with the examination of the correlates of departmental attempts to influence arrest discretion. In situations such as this where the research focus is on examining the impact of several independent variables on a single dependent, multiple regression is the appropriate analysis technique. This approach is used as a means of quantifying both the amount of variance in the Arrest Discretion Control Scale (ADCS) explained by all of the independent variables acting together and the relative importance of each independent variable as an influence on the dependent variable (Blalock, 1982).

CHAPTER 4

How Police Agencies Attempt to Influence Discretion

This chapter presents the findings and results of the data analysis of the research questions presented in Chapter 3. For purposes of this research, two general empirical tasks were undertaken. First an examination of the conceptual nature of police organizations influence on arrest discretion was conducted as a means of creating a scale to measure the extent to which department's attempted to control or affect arrest discretion. The initial part of this chapter reports on the empirical performance of this multi-dimensional measure as a way of capturing the extent of department interest in influencing arrest discretion. The second empirical task undertaken focuses upon examining the relationships of the variables identified as correlates of attempted control of arrest discretion. In Chapter 3, an expected direction was specified for the relationship of each of the four correlates with the Arrest Discretion Control Scale (ADCS).

The first section of this chapter reports the characteristics of the police departments for which questionnaires were returned. In this study, all variables are measured at the organizational level, since police departments were the unit of analysis. This information is categorized by State, and the size of the sworn officer population within the organization. The next section of this chapter addresses research question one by calculating and showing the distribution of police departments along the Arrest Discretion Control Scale (ADCS), including simple scale item analysis. The remainder of the chapter is organized around a regression analysis to address the four remaining research questions, each of which addresses one of the theoretically defined correlates of arrest discretion. This chapter will focus on the simple presentation of findings in a brief form; elaboration and more extensive interpretation of the results will be presented in Chapter 5.

The Police Departments Studied

There are 211 municipal police departments in the United States with 200 or more sworn police officers. Since the complete population of interest was manageable, a census of the entire population of departments was undertaken rather than a sample. Unlike the case with random sampling, there are no specific guidelines about completion rates when taking a census. Certainly, any completion rate less than 100% attenuates the connection between the reported data and the population. On the other hand, perfect participation rates are virtually impossible to achieve. Two guidelines are traditionally followed with censuses. The first is adopted from survey sampling and suggests that a minimum completion rate of 60.0% is generally acceptable for the meaningful analysis of data (Babbie, 1998). The second strategy used in censuses is to carefully specify the characteristics of the population that returned the questionnaires as a means of clarifying participation for the reader. Of the 211 municipal police departments surveyed, 147 (70%) completed and returned the instrument, leaving 64 (30%) that did not. This completion rate is well above the minimum return rate of 60.0% found to be acceptable for similar methodologies and research designs. Table 2 shows the state in which the police departments that did and did not participate in the study were located.

Table 2. Comparison of Police Departments by State Between Respondents and Nonrespondents

State	Number Sent	Number Returned	Percent Returned
Alabama	5	1	20%
Alaska	1	0	0%
Arizona	6	6	100%
Arkansas	1	1	100%
California	27	22	81%
Colorado	4	4	100%
Connecticut	5	2	40%
Delaware	1	0	0%
District of Columbia	1	1	100%
Florida	16	13	81%
Georgia	6	5	83%
Hawaii	1	1	100%
Idaho	1	1	100%

Table 2 Continued

Illinois	6	5	83%
Indiana	6	4	67%
Iowa	1	1	100%
Kansas	4	4	100%
Kentucky	2	2	100%
Louisiana	4	2	50%
Massachusetts	8	4	50%
Michigan	7	6	86%
Minnesota	2	1	50%
Mississippi	1	1	100%
Missouri	3	3	100%
Nebraska	2	2	100%
Nevada	2	1	50%
New Jersey	8	4	50%
New Mexico	1	1	100%
New York	6	3	50%
North Carolina	8	6	75%
Ohio	8	4	50%
Oklahoma	2	2	100%
Oregon	1	1	100%
Pennsylvania	5	3	60%
Rhode Island	1	0	0%
South Carolina	3	3	100%
Tennessee	5	5	100%
Texas	18	13	72%
Utah	1	1	100%
Virginia	15	6	40%
Washington	3	1	33%
Wisconsin	3	1	33%

In this study 41 states and the District of Columbia are represented, of which 18 of these states had a 100% return rate. Only three states (Alaska, Delaware, and Rhode Island) where each had one survey sent, failed to respond. Twenty-one states had a partial response to the surveys sent, the lowest percentage from Alabama (20%) and the highest percentage from Michigan (86%). California had the highest number of surveys sent (27) and returned (22) for a return rate of 81%.

While the overall participation rate is high, a more noticeable trend in response is provided in the breakdown of agency size and region. Table 3 provides a breakdown of agencies by number of sworn personnel, the number of survey instruments sent to these agencies, and the response rate. The majority of police departments in the United States are considerably small by comparison, so it was not unexpected to have a majority of surveys (35%) sent to agencies with 300 or fewer personnel. This size category had the largest raw number of surveys sent and returned. Of course, the smallest number of surveys (<1%) went to the largest agencies, those with more than 3000 personnel. Of these large agencies only one, New York City, failed to respond with a survey. The highest percentage of returns came from agencies that fell into the median category (1001-1500), with an 89% return rate. The lowest percentage return was provided by the second smallest size category (301-500), with a return rate of 62%. These data indicate that completion rates for all size categories are significantly representative.

Table 3. Police Departments by Number of Sworn Officers (size) Showing Respondents and Nonrespondents

Number of Sworn Officers	Number Sent	Number Returned	Percent Returned
200-300	73	47	64%
301-500	61	38	62%
501-1000	37	30	81%
1001-1500	18	16	89%
1501-2000	9	7	78%
2001-3000	8	5	63%
>3000	7	6	86%

In addition to size, respondents were broken down into one of five regions of the United States: Northeast, Southeast, Midwest, Southwest, and West. These regions are based, in part, on FBI Uniform Crime Reporting Area Definitions. For purposes of this study the investigator further refined the four major UCR regions into five areas that provide increased specificity for survey responses. The following identifies each region and the states included for this research. **Northeast:** Maryland, Pennsylvania, New York, New Jersey, Connecticut, Massachusetts, Vermont, Rhode Island, New Hampshire, Maine and Washington DC. **Southeast:** Arkansas, Louisiana,

Mississippi, Alabama, Georgia, Florida, South Carolina, North Carolina, Virginia, West Virginia, Kentucky, and Tennessee. **Midwest:** Minnesota, Wisconsin, Michigan, Indiana, Ohio, Illinois, Iowa, Missouri, Kansas, Nebraska, South Dakota, and North Dakota. **Southwest:** Texas, New Mexico, Arizona, and Oklahoma. **West:** Montana, Wyoming, Colorado, Utah, Nevada, Idaho, California, Oregon, Washington, Hawaii, and Alaska.

Table 4 shows the number of surveys sent and returned within each region. The highest percentage of return rates came from the Midwest and Southwest regions (81%), while the lowest rate of return was from the Northeast region (50%). The highest number of surveys sent (66) went to the Southeast, and the lowest (27) went to the Southwest.

Table 4. Police Departments by United States Region Showing Surveys Sent and Those Returned

Region	Number Sent	Number Returned	Percent Returned
Northeast	34	17	50%
Southeast	66	45	68%
Midwest	42	34	81%
Southwest	27	22	81%
West	41	32	78%

In an effort to motivate a respondent response to the survey, each agency was asked on the survey instrument if they desired to have a copy of the completed research summary. This technique is part of Dillman's (1978) "total design method" that is used to provide inducements for higher return rates. Table 5 shows a breakdown by region of the number of returned surveys and those requesting the research summary. The highest number of requests for the research summary came from the Southeast (31) and the highest percentage of requests came from the Southwest (73%). The lowest number of requests came from the Northeast (7) that, in addition, was the region with the lowest percentage of requests (41%) for the research summary. Interestingly, the Midwest had one of the highest return rates (81%) for surveys, but had one of the lower request rates (56%) for the research summary.

Table 5. Police Departments by United States Region Showing
Requests for Research Summary

Region	Number Returned	Requests for Research	Percent Requesting Research
Northeast	17	7	41%
Southeast	45	31	69%
Midwest	34	19	56%
Southwest	22	16	73%
West	32	21	66%

Since only departments with 200 or more sworn officers were used, any knowledge of smaller police departments is precluded from this study. This raises the issue of validity as to whether research results will apply to smaller agencies, non-municipal agencies, and those that reside outside the United States. The population for this study was restricted to such law enforcement agencies described above for practicality purposes. Since the focus of research is on the arrest decision process and discretion, the main thrust in the sampling frame was to expose those agencies with a more significant number of arrest incidents. Theoretically, it is believed that organizational structures and styles that influence control of discretion in median to large police departments will apply to smaller law enforcement agencies in the United States. While similar results may be found in police agencies in developed countries, it is unclear how such results would apply in undeveloped countries.

Arrest Discretion Control Scale

Prior to the collection of data, the Arrest Discretion Control Scale was pretested for reliability using a "test-retest" technique (Edwards, 1957). Twelve sworn officers from the Phoenix and Tempe Police Departments were used as the group on which the scale was pre-tested. The participants in the test-retest were at the rank of Commander or higher and understood their department's arrest policies, procedures, and training. After the scale was administered, the order of presentation of items was randomized and the scale was re-administered to the same group seven days later. The time required for each person to complete the questionnaire was recorded and comments on each question were solicited. The Pearson's Product-moment correlation between the first administration and the second administration was $r^2 = .816$. Using Edwards' (1957) criterion that correlations above .80 represent acceptable reliability, the Arrest Discretion Control Scale was determined to be reliable. After the data were collected, a routine Scale Item Analysis (Edwards, 1957) was performed on the twenty items that composed the ADCS scale. The purpose of scale item analysis is to verify that a constructed scale contains items that are statistically additive as shown by statistics indicating that they are not highly intercorrelated with one another, thereby giving evidence that they are in fact measuring different scale dimensions.

In the scale item analysis no pair of items displayed a correlation coefficient higher than .59. The normal statistical threshold for item intercorrelations is that pairs of items used in the same scale should not produce a Pearson's r coefficient higher than .75 (Lewis-Beck, 1980). Furthermore, the single item intraclass correlation coefficient (ICC) for the scale was .21. The ICC approximates the average correlation across all items and item colinearity is considered problematic only if the coefficient magnitude exceeds .5. Based on these statistics, one can conclude that the Arrest Discretion Control Scale items are additive. In addition to the test-retest reliability reported above, the value of Cronbach's Alpha calculated as part of the item analysis was $\alpha=.77$. Alpha is a measure of scale reproducibility, commonly used as an indicator of reliability; values above .70 are considered to indicate a reliable scale (Edwards, 1957).

Agency Influence of Arrest Discretion

In keeping with the description in Chapter 3, the Likert scale measuring Police Department attempts to influence arrest discretion (ADCS scale) contains 20 statements reflecting the dimensions of interest. Responses to this scale were coded such that the lowest levels of attempted discretion control correspond with the lower numerical anchor of the scale (1.0), and the highest levels are represented by the upper numerical anchor point (6.0). Each item was expressed in classic Likert format on the questionnaire as a statement — for example, "This department has extensive written policies governing the procedures for arrest" — and given the same response format to describe the intensity of respondent agreement in one of six categories: Strongly Agree,

Agree, Somewhat Agree, Somewhat Disagree, Disagree, Strongly Disagree. Again, the coding scheme is such that increased levels of agreement indicate that procedures, protocols and guidelines exist that attempt to shape or control officer arrest discretion. All summated ratings scales produce a range of scale values that match the category descriptors used for the response format. Thus, for the Arrest Discretion Control Scale (ADCS), a scale score of 1.0 indicates that the department has none of the twenty procedures or protocols described in the items. Similarly, scale scores near 2.0 show that the department had few of the twenty guidelines and rules specified. Each subsequent scale anchor (3,4,5,6) represents increasing attention to influencing arrest discretion, with 6.0 being the upper limit of maximum attempted departmental control.

Table 6 shows the distribution of police departments by grouped score on the Arrest Discretion Control Scale (ADCS). The lowest observed score was 2.90 (indicating that on the whole, the department used a few of the protocols, procedures and guidelines specified in the scale), and this score was seen for only one department.

Table 6. Arrest Discretion Control Scale (ADCS) Score Summary

Scale Value	Number	Percent
< 2.50	0	0
2.50 – 2.99	1	.7
3.00 – 3.49	6	4.3
3.50 – 3.99	23	16.7
4.00 – 4.49	40	29.0
4.50 – 4.99	48	34.8
5.00 – 5.49	17	12.3
5.50 – 6.00	3	2.2

Note. Range of scores was 2.90 through 5.65. The mean score was 4.41. The median was 4.45. The Standard Deviation was .55.

The highest score was 5.65 (indicating that the department used nearly all twenty of the specified protocols, procedures and guidelines to attempt to shape arrest discretion) and one department also achieved this score. Thus, the scale scores actually obtained for departments run across most of the six anchor points of scores that are theoretically possible. This suggests there is substantial variation — relative to the scale dimensions — in how much police departments attempt to control arrest discretion.

When one examines the distribution of departments on the discretion scale, it is clear that most departments actively attempt to limit or at least delimit officer discretion in making arrests. The average score on the scale was 4.41, placing the average department well above the midpoint of the scale. The median of the scores was 4.45 and the standard deviation was .55; in combination with the mean, these statistics reaffirm that the majority of departments are concentrated in the scale scores ranging from 3.5 through 4.99. The concentration of departments on the upper end of the arrest discretion scale reinforces the idea that arrests are very important issues for police departments and that considerable organizational energy is expended in trying to influence the ways in which street officers handle the activity. Indeed, only two departments show scale scores that are at or below the midpoint of the scale (3.0), while 78.3% of the departments are at or above the score of 4.0.

In Chapter 3, arrest discretion views (and hence the scale) were conceived to reflect four different dimensions. The research literature indicates that the way an organization creates a structure for arrest discretion flows from these four principal sources: *official policy, process, training, and values*. These dimensions capture the channels through which organizational management can attempt to influence or constrain the arrest behavior of officers. It is crucial to remember that the issue in measurement of organizational constraints on officer discretion is *not the absolute amount of discretion* that is permitted. Instead, the focus is upon the extent to which the *organization attempts to control* the exercise of discretion, where discretion is characterized as the ability of the officer to deviate from department procedures and norms.

The policy dimension is associated with every organization and it is particularly important among social control agencies. Policy has long been considered one of the most effective methods in guiding professional police judgment. The process dimension involves the department's attempt to influence officer discretion in the *procedural requirements* associated with making arrests. This process dimension involves organizational imposition of procedures that must be followed for officers to effect an arrest. The process dimension includes structural processes that are in place to enhance professional judgment, correct deficiencies, or serve as a warning device to potential problems in unwarranted discretion. The third dimension of organizational influence on officer discretion addresses the issue of *training*. In all organizations, training represents the chief way in which policy and procedures are translated into behavior expectations for employees. Training also insures that employees have the elemental ability to execute the organizational expectations. The last dimension of the extent to which department's attempt to constrain arrest processes addresses the notion of departmental *values*. This dimension represents an attempt to capture the effects of police culture on the practice of arrests by officers. It is argued that the professional ethos of the organization sets the tone for its members. As police agencies work on developing relationships with the community, police executives need to find ways to guide discretion and police behavior generally through increasing reliance on values instead of relying strictly on rules and protocols of accountability.

Because these dimensions were conceptually separated and different Likert items were associated with each dimension, one can create them as specific scales to reflect the underlying ideas of each dimension. Table 7 shows the basic statistics for each dimension when constructed as a Likert scale containing the five items specified in chapter 3. The data in table 7 suggest that most departments make significant attempts to control arrest discretion through each of the dimensional areas identified. Both policy and process mechanisms were found to reach significant mean scale values (4.58 and 4.56 respectively) with three departments scoring at the highest anchor point (6.0) in the policy dimension, and four departments scoring 6.0 in the process dimension. One department scored a low 1.20 in the policy dimension, which was the lowest scale score of all the dimension categories. The charge that law enforcement agencies are comprised of rigid, militaristic structures, would seem to validate high scores in the policy and process arena. On the other hand, training is usually argued to be one of the most costly and time competitive components of a police organization, one in which it was expected that departments may avoid for discretion control. However, the training component, which has been routinely criticized as one of the most neglected areas of law enforcement, especially in the arrest process (Davis, 1975), surprisingly was found to have the highest mean scale value (4.63). This indicates that across the departments studied, the five indicators of training averaged a level of attention well above the midpoint of the scale. In fact, eight departments scored the highest score (upper anchor point) available on the ADCS scale (6.0). This was higher than any other dimensional category.

Table 7. Summary Statistics for Dimensional Scales

Dimension	Mean	Median	SD	Low Score (# Of Depts.)	High Score (# Of Depts.)
Policy	4.58	4.80	.81	1.20 (1)	6.00 (3)
Process	4.56	4.80	.87	2.20 (2)	6.00 (4)
Training	4.63	4.80	.88	2.20 (2)	6.00 (8)
Values	3.85	3.80	.64	2.20 (3)	5.40 (1)

Finally, values issues were used as arrest control strategies less often than any other dimension based measure. The mean score for use of values was 3.85 (the median was 3.80, with a standard deviation of .64). This score places the use of values approaches slightly above the midpoint of the scale, suggesting that the five indicators of values (independence, professionalism, citizen review, community policing, and relationship to management) are seen as acceptable means of influencing arrest discretion. Conversely, this does raise the question of the community policing philosophy and its inroads into contemporary law enforcement. The median and mean scores for each of the dimensional scales are similar in magnitude and the standard deviations are small, indicating there is little spread among the departments on these mean ratings.

Ultimately, however, the measures that are seen as most acceptable, and presumably most efficacious, in influencing arrest discretion lie in the realm of training. The five policy indicators were having a comprehensive field-training program, frequent arrest procedure training, training for supervisors, training in making discretionary choices, and monitoring the effectiveness of such training. Close behind were the dimensional categories of policy and process.

Correlates of Department Influence on Arrest Discretion

Chapter 3 asks the following research question, " What is the relationship between organizational bureaucracy and the influence on police officer discretion in field arrests?" For purposes of this study, bureaucracy is operationalized as the number of levels of management between the police chief and line-level officers, and the number of divisions within the department. It is believed that highly bureaucratic departments become focused on a "conception of order," meaning strict compliance with rules and regulations. Table 8 illustrates that 11 departments (7.5%) maintained seven or more levels of command, while 35 departments (23.8%) had six levels of command. While no agencies had two or fewer supervisory levels, only three agencies (2%) maintained three levels of supervision. Twenty-six agencies (17.7%) had four levels of command, and the majority of police departments surveyed, 71 (48.3%) had five levels of command. Across all the departments studied, the mean number of supervisory levels was 4.17 (standard deviation = 0.88). The zero-order or bi-variate Pearson's product-moment correlation of number of supervisory levels with the Arrest Discretion Control Scale yielded a squared coefficient of 0.19 ($p<.05$). This statistically significant coefficient indicates that there is a positive relationship between number of supervisory levels and department intentions to control arrest discretion. Specifically, number of supervision levels explains nineteen percent of the variance in the ADCS.

Table 8. Number of Supervisory Levels Within the Organization

Number of Supervisor Levels	Number	Percent
2 or Fewer Levels	0	0
3 Levels	3	2.0
4 Levels	26	17.7
5 Levels	71	48.3
6 Levels	35	23.8
7 or More Levels	11	7.5

Table 9 breaks down agency respondents into the number of work divisions found in their organization. In Chapter 3 we use work divisions as part of the operational definition of bureaucracy. Therefore, it is postulated that the higher the bureaucratic composition of a police department the greater will be the organizational attempt to influence discretionary decision making regarding field arrests. Table 9 shows that one-third of the departments maintained nine or more divisions; this is the largest single proportion among all of the categories of numbers of divisions. The second largest proportion of departments (31.3%) reported having 3 or 4 divisions. The next largest grouping maintained either 5 or 6 divisions, and nearly eleven percent of the departments reported having 7 or 8 divisions.

Table 9. Number of Work Divisions Within the Police Department

Number of Divisions	Number	Percent
1-2 Divisions	1	.7
3-4 Divisions	46	31.3
5-6 Divisions	34	23.1
7-8 Divisions	16	10.9
9 or More Divisions	49	33.3

Only 1 department reported having fewer than 3 divisions. Thus, there is a bi-modal quality to the distribution, with about one-third of the departments having a large number of divisions and an almost equal proportion maintaining 3 or 4 divisions. Overall, ignoring the category groupings, the mean number of divisions is 4.45 (standard deviation = 1.27). The Pearson's product-moment correlation coefficient squared for number of divisions with the Arrest Discretion Control Scale is − 0.18 (p<.05). This coefficient indicates that there is a negative relationship between the number of divisions and attempts to constrain arrest decision-making; the number of divisions explains eighteen percent of the variance in the arrest discretion control scale. As stated in chapter 3, it was expected that the higher the bureaucratic composition of a police department the more significant will be the organizational influence over discretionary decision making regarding field arrests. The disparity in this hypothesis is discussed in detail in chapter 5.

Organizational Professionalism

In Chapter 3 the issue of organizational professionalism and the relationship with discretion control of police officer arrests is raised. The aspects of organizational professionalism selected for exploration in this research include (1) the amount of entry level education required for police officers to be a member of the department, and (2) the number of specialty units within the department. While past studies have produced varied and confusing results (Smith and Klein, 1983) regarding the effect of professionalism on the arrest decision process, commitment to education and the orientation to community service (specialized units) is expected to increase the flexibility of discretionary choices for police officers. It is hypothesized that the higher the level of professionalism for a department the lower the level of organizational control over discretionary arrest decisions.

Table 10 indicates the breakdown of entry-level education required of police officers that are hired onto the department. Treating these categories as a group of ordinal-scaled education descriptors numbered from none (1) through more than a bachelor's degree (6), the mean category across the departments is the second category (high school education). The standard deviation of .89 reflects the distribution in the table, indicating that most of the cases lie in this category. The Pearson's product-moment correlation coefficient (squared) for entry level required education with the arrest discretion scale is 0.10 (p>.05). This indicates that while education entry requirements are positively correlated with the ADCS, education requirements only explain ten percent of the variance in the ADCS, and that the relationship is not statistically significant.

Table 10. Entry Level Education Within the Police Department

Level of Education	Number	Percent
None	0	0
HS/GED	104	70.7
Some College	15	10.2
2yr College	22	15.0
4yr Degree	6	4.1
Above 4yr Degree	0	0

It should be pointed out that the relatively low correlation of education might be a function of the lack of variation among departments on the entry-level educational requirement. With more than 70 percent of the departments in the same category (high school education), there is little variation on this variable that is available to explain variation in the arrest discretion control scale. It is possible that a different sample wherein departments had more varied entrance requirements would show a higher magnitude of correlation.

Table 11 illustrates the number of specialty details within a police department. The mean number of specialty details was found to be 9.4 (standard deviation = 1.79).

Table 11. Number of Specialty Details Within the Police Department

Number of Specialty Details	Number	Percent
4 Details	3	2.0
5 Details	1	.7
6 Details	8	5.4
7 Details	8	5.4
8 Details	15	10.2
9 Details	33	22.4
10 Details	37	25.2
11 Details	29	19.7
12 Details	13	8.8

The Pearson's product-moment correlation coefficient squared for the relationship between number of specialty details and the arrest discretion control scale is 0.16 ($p<.05$). Consequently, as the number of specialty details increase so does a department's attempt to reduce independent decision making regarding arrests.

Department Size

Department size can be measured in a variety of ways, however, for purposes of this research size will relate to the number of sworn (police officers) personnel in the department. This research asks the question of how organizational size impacts the degree of influence over police officer discretion in field arrests. It is postulated that the measures of size will be inversely correlated with police officer discretion.

Research is mixed on the impact of department size on discretionary decisions to arrest. Mastrofski, Ritti, and Hoffmaster (1987) found that officers in smaller departments were more likely to arrest than their larger department counterparts. The willingness of officers to arrest decreased as department size and level of bureaucracy increased. However, Brown (1988) found that officers in large departments experienced more latitude and autonomy and were more inclined to act (arrest). There is the presumption that large departments have less effective controls on their members, less group stability, and a weaker link to the community that tends to subtract from the service style of policing. This makes it difficult to describe whether the relationship of size will have a direct or inverse relationship with discretionary influence.

Table 12 breaks down the number of sworn personnel for the agency into seven categories. As was anticipated, the majority of respondent agencies were in the smallest category of sworn officers with 47 agencies (32%) having 300 or fewer personnel. The number of agencies progressively decreases with the increase in sworn personnel. Only six departments (4.1%) constitute the largest agencies, with more than 3000 sworn personnel. The mean category for number of sworn officers is 2.48 (standard deviation = 1.62). This score indicates that the balance point of the distribution of categories lies between the grouping for 301-500 personnel and the grouping for 501-1000 personnel.

Table 12. Number of Sworn Officers in the Department

Number of Sworn Officers	Number	Percent
≤ 300	47	32.0
301-500	38	25.9
501-1000	30	20.4
1001-1500	16	10.9
1501-2000	7	4.8
2001-3000	5	3.4
> 3000	6	4.1

The Pearson's r^2 for the relationship between number of sworn officers and the arrest discretion control scale is -.03 (p>.05). This indicates that at the bi-variate level, there is no statistically significant relationship between category of sworn officers and the ADCS.

Supervisory Span of Control

In this study, supervisory span of control focuses on the span of control for field (street) supervisors. One obvious way a supervisor has of influencing discretion and maintaining some control over patrol officers is simply by being present at the scene of a call. Those police departments that have a high number of officers for each supervisor are expected to have less effective controls on their members. Interestingly, some research found that the presence of police supervisors increased the likelihood of arrest. Smith and Klein (1983) found that militaristic and legalistic departments, especially, produced more arrests when an on-scene supervisor was present. Kelling argues that in today's litigious society, along with the risk of discipline involved in improper arrest procedures, that officers are more likely to avoid arrest situations if at all possible. Lack of supervision can enhance such avoidance.

For purposes of this study, supervision is operationalized as the number of patrol officers normally assigned to one field supervisor, keeping in mind that many agencies have policy limits on span of control even though the actual numbers may fluctuate slightly. Table 13 shows agency responses to specified categories of police officers assigned to one street supervisor. The smallest category involved the largest number of officers (14+) assigned to one supervisor and included two agencies (1.4%). The largest categorical response was in the 6-7 officer grouping, which included 68 agencies (46.3%). The next highest grouping involved forty-eight agencies (32.7%) that responded in the 8-9 officer category. In addition, both the five or less category and the 12-13 officer category had eight agencies respond, or 5.4% of the respondents. Thirteen agencies, or 8.8% of the respondents, marked the 10-11 officer grouping. Taking the described categories as a set of ordinal groupings, the mean category values is 2.67, placing it between 6-7 officers and 8-9 officers (standard deviation = 1.01).

Table 13. Supervisory Span of Control Within the Police Department

# of Officers Per Supervisor	Number	Percent
5 or Less	8	5.4
6-7 Officers	68	46.3
8-9 Officers	48	32.7
10-11 Officers	13	8.8
12-13 Officers	8	5.4
14 or More	2	1.4

The Pearson's r^2 for the relationship of span of control with the arrest discretion control scale is .21 (P<.05). Thus, there is a statistically significant, positive correlation wherein span of control explains 21 percent of the variance in the ADCS.

Regression Analysis

Chapter 3 focused upon defining a number of correlates of department attempts to influence officer arrest discretion. These correlates can be treated as independent variables and include: (1) organizational bureaucracy, (2) professionalism, as indicated by educational entry standards and the number of specialty units offered in the department, (3) department size, and (4) supervisory load. It is appropriate to conceive of these independent variables in conjunction with the dependent variable of arrest discretion scale score as a simple single stage regression model. Thus, the following discussion will examine the independent variables and their relationships to one another and to the dependent variable. Regression analysis provides coefficients so that the researcher may assess the independent contributions of each independent variable to explaining the dependent variable, while taking into account (or controlling for) the effects of each of the other independent variables (Heise, 1975).

Multiple regression (like the analysis of variance and covariance) is a technique based upon the general linear model of statistics (Mosteller and Tukey, 1977). This statistical system is designed to examine the relationships among a number of independent variables and one dependent variable. Multiple regression answers two questions about any statistical model: what is the relative importance of the independent variables in causing change in the dependent variable, and how much variance in the dependent variable is explained by all of the independent variables acting together (Mosteller and Tukey, 1977). The relative importance of the independent variables is assessed using the standardized partial regression coefficient, also known as a beta (β) coefficient (Matlack, 1993). The beta statistic is calculated for each predictor variable. It is interpreted as the amount of change in the dependent variable associated with a standardized one-unit change in the focal independent variable, controlling for the effects of all other independent variables. Beta coefficients vary between a lower anchor value of -1.0 and an upper limit of $+1.0$, with the sign indicating the direction of the relationship between the focal independent variable and the dependent variable (Blalock, 1982).

The relative importance of predictor variables is evaluated by comparing the magnitude of the beta coefficients (Matlack, 1993) for different predictors. The higher the coefficient value, the greater the amount of unique change caused in the dependent variable by the focal predictor. Consequently, the greater the amount of change in the dependent variable, the greater the relative importance of that independent variable. There is some disagreement and statisticians urge caution in making such inferences literal in interpretation or attributing great precision to the meaning of differences in beta coefficients. Lewis-Beck (1980) points out that the magnitude of beta coefficients is affected by factors other than the "true" relationship between the predictor and the dependent variable. Thus, beta values can be attenuated (made larger or smaller) in the presence of multi-colinearity, if the theoretical model fails to include all important predictor variables (specification error), or in the presence of large measurement errors (scale unreliability) (Duncan, 1975). As Lewis-Beck (1980) argues, however, in spite of these other influences on beta magnitude, beta coefficients are universally used as the basis for ranking the relative importance of predictor variables. If in practice, analysts carefully construct their conceptual model, carefully screen for measure unreliability, and screen for the presence of multi-colinearity, then beta coefficients can be meaningfully interpreted (Blalock, 1982).

Beta coefficients are tested for statistical significance. A Student's t statistic (Knoke and Bohrnstedt, 1994) is calculated to assess the probability that the observed beta coefficient is not statistically significant from a value of zero. Since beta measures the amount of change in the dependent variable, a value of zero would indicate that the predictor had no impact on the dependent variable. Statistically, beta values that are not statistically significant are probably not producing a large enough change in the dependent variable to be substantively (theoretically) important.

The second question answered by regression addresses the total impact of all the predictors on the dependent variable. This is accomplished by examining the multiple correlation coefficient R, which serves as a measure of explained variance in the dependent variable. It has been long known that R is difficult to interpret because of inherent ambiguity in the assignment of meaning to coefficient values (Morrison, 1976). Mueller, Schussler, and Costner (1977) developed a proportional reduction in error interpretation for R that involves alternately focusing on the squared value of the coefficient. In this formulation, R^2 can be interpreted as the amount of variance in the dependent variable that is explained by all predictor variables acting together. Values of R^2 range between zero (no variance explained) and 1.0 (indicating that 100 percent of the variance is explained). This statistic has no positive or negative sign because it represents the total variance explained by all of the independent variables, some of which may be positively and others negatively related to the dependent variable. This statistic is commonly used as a measure of the "goodness of fit" of a given data set to a specific model. The multiple correlation coefficient squared is also tested for statistical significance. The F-ratio is used for this test because it allows a means of assessing the difference between the observed explained variance (R^2) and a value of zero (where zero indicates that the predictors—collectively— explain no variance).

As indicated above when beta values were discussed, the application of regression analysis makes assumptions about the nature of the data being analyzed. The extent to which the data do not fit the assumptions constrain the interpretation of the regression analysis. Two assumptions not addressed above are that the relationships in the model being analyzed are assumed to be linear and that the scales of all variables in the analysis can be treated as if they were interval (Horton, 1985). Virtually all statistics assume or are capable of detecting only linear relationships. Because this is the case, relationships among independent and dependent variables to be used in a multiple regression analysis are routinely displayed at the bi-variate level and inspected to detect evidence of nonlinear relationships. Of course, when a model is formed, if there is a substantial theoretical reason to believe some predictor may have a nonlinear (curvilinear) relationship to the dependent variable, regression analysis would either be eliminated as a technique, or the predictor could be transformed (by taking a log of the values) into a linear predictor (Blalock, 1982). In this case, there were no theoretical reasons to suspect curvilinear relationships. All of the variables used in the model examined here are measured as ordinal categories. The use of ordinal variables as if they were interval has long been considered acceptable for regression analysis (Blalock, 1964). Boyle (1970), using simulation methods, demonstrated that regression analysis is robust for violations of the interval measurement assumption, but more importantly, determined that for linear regression an ordinal variable with 5 or more categories did not perform differently than an interval variable.

A third assumption in regression analysis is that the predictor variables are not intercorrelated. This assumption is considered critical in regression analysis because the presence of such intercorrelation— referred to as multicollinearity—causes significant difficulty in interpreting coefficients. This *multicollinearity* means that you may not be able to tell the influence of one independent variable free from the influence of the independent variables with which it is correlated.

The objective in regression analysis is to examine the interrelationships of the predictor variables to determine if such multi-colinearity is present. High intercorrelations among predictor variables can cause beta coefficients and the multiple regression coefficient to exceed their upper limits, this makes meaningful interpretation impossible (Neter, Wasserman and Kutner, 1985). There are many approaches to assessing the presence of multicollinearity. The most commonly used approach involves inspecting the observed intercorrelations of the predictors to insure that none are too high and inspecting the beta and R values to insure that they are within prescribed range for each coefficient (Lewis-Beck, 1980).

Table 14 shows the means, standard deviations and zero order correlation coefficients for the six variables chosen as predictors of departmental influence on arrest discretion. By examining means and standard deviations one can determine that sufficient variation is present to avoid the problem of "statistical restriction of range," wherein a variable is so constricted that it approaches the status of a constant (Neter, Wasserman and Kutner, 1985). In this case, all of the predictors show reasonable variation as measured by the standard deviations; only required years of education required to apply for a police job and number of supervisory levels have standard deviations of less than one category. The correlations among predictors as measured by Pearson's product-moment correlation coefficient squared (r^2) for the most part show very low magnitudes, indicating a lack of multi-colinearity. The highest observed correlation is between number of specialty details offered by the department and size of the department as indicated by the number of sworn officers, producing an $r^2 = .43$.

Table 14. Predictor Summary Statistics and Correlations

Variable	Mean	SD	(1)	(2)	(3)	(4)	(5)	(6)
Span (1)	2.65	1.01	-	.15[a]	.04	.17[a]	-.00	-.09
Divisions(2)	4.48	1.26	-	-	.12	.28[a]	.12	.01
Supervise (3)	4.28	0.88	-	-	-	.38[a]	.12	-.02
Sworn(4)	2.55	1.59	-	-	-	-	.43[a]	.00
Specialty (5)	9.38	1.81	-	-	-	-	-	-.09
Education (6)	2.51	0.89	-	-	-	-	-	-

Note. [a]p<.05

Substantively, it is reasonable to expect that these two variables would be correlated, since each variable is related to resources available in a law enforcement department. Lewis-Beck (1980) argues that zero order correlation levels need to be above .8 before any multicollinearity consequences arise. Since the beta and R values are within range (see Table 15) and the predictor intercorrelations are below the threshold value of .8, one can conclude from these analyses that multicollinearity is not a problem in this dataset.

Table 15 shows the regression summary statistics for the analysis of the model with six predictors (supervisor span of control, number of divisions in the department, number of supervisory levels, number of sworn personnel, the number of specialty details in the department, and level of education required for job application) and the dependent variable of score on the Arrest Discretion Control Scale. The R^2 value indicates that all of these predictors together explain 20 percent of the variance in the ADCS scale, and that this value is statistically significant at the $p < .01$ level.

Table 15. Regression Summary Statistics

Predictor	Beta (β)[a]	t Statistic	Probability of t
Span of control	-.17	-2.1	.03
Divisions	-.13	-.16	.10
Supervisory Levels	.25	3.0	.003
Number Sworn Personnel	-.31	-3.2	.001
Number Specialty Details	.22	2.5	.01
Education	.14	1.8	.07

Note. $F_{6,134} = 5.5$, $p < .01$. R=.44; $R^2 = .20$
[a]Standardized Partial Regression Coefficient

Thus, one may conclude that the model developed in this study has a good fit to the data; while variance is left unexplained, the predictors account for one-fifth of the variance in scale score. The significance of the F ratio indicates that this proportion of explained variance is unlikely to have been caused by random variation. The beta statistics reveal the amount of change in the dependent variable caused by the focal predictor variable while controlling for all of the other predictors. Although it is not a measure of explained variance, the larger a beta value, the more important is the predictor. Beta statistics that are not statistically significant ($p > .05$) are not causing enough change in the dependent variable to be substantively important. Using this criterion, four of the six predictors are statistically significant. In chapter 3, it was argued that larger departments would have lower scores on the Arrest Discretion Control Scale. Those police departments that have a high number of officers are expected to have less effective controls on their members. The data confirm this expectation, with number of sworn personnel generating a statistically significant beta value of -.31 (P< .01).

It was expected that the level of professionalism in the department—represented by specialty details and educational requirements—would be inversely related to the level of attempted influence on arrest discretion. The data indicate that each of these expectations was not correct. The number of specialty details shows a statistically significant beta value of .22, indicating that as the number of programs increase, so does the department's score on the Arrest Discretion Control Scale. Similarly, the presence of educational entrance requirements is positively related to Arrest Discretion Control Scale score, with a beta of .14, but this value is not statistically significant (p> .05). It was also expected that as departments became more bureaucratic, concerns with influencing arrest discretion would increase. Two measures of bureaucracy—number of divisions and number of levels of command—were used. The number of divisions was, as expected, negatively related to score on the arrest discretion scale with a beta of -.13. Unfortunately, this beta coefficient was not large enough to be statistically reliable (p>.05). Number of supervisory levels was statistically significantly related to the ADCS score, and the relationship was large and positive as hypothesized (beta= .25, p <.01).

Finally, supervisor span of control was expected to be positively related to departmental levels of influence over arrest discretion. Those police departments that have a high ratio of officers for each patrol supervisor were expected to have less effective controls on their members. Span of control generated a beta of -.17, indicating that as the number of officers assigned to one supervisor increases, the department score on the influencing arrest discretion scale decreases. Thus, as supervisors are spread more thinly — covering more officers — the extent of departmental attempts to influence arrest discretion are reduced.

The Implications for Law Enforcement Practitioners

Chapter 5 is an opportunity to move beyond the data and integrate the results of this study with existing theory and research. A significant presumption of this research has been that street-level discretion by field officers can be affected by organizational structures. The importance of the arrest decision in the field (patrol), and how the organization influences such discretion provides the focus for this research. Thus, conceptual interest is in defining discretion in arrest decisions that flow from structural, procedural, and attitudinal features of a department. While there has been considerable research focus placed on individual, situational, and even community level indicators regarding police discretionary behavior, little has been done in the area of organizational effects. A review of the literature strongly suggests that such organizational indicators can have a significant impact on influencing such areas as police decision-making, which includes the decision to arrest or not to arrest.

Police discretion exists when officers have some leeway or choice in how to respond to a situation. The fewer the rules about handling incidents and situations, the more discretion officers can exercise. A review of the literature found only modest empirical research testing the association of organizational structures and the arrest decision process. However, the literature was essential in elucidating dimensions of police work and the complexity of how police respond to situations. Of significance, and noted early on, is that police discretion is inescapable. The real challenge for law enforcement organizations is how to control and guide discretion so that officers have the flexibility to make timely decisions in real-world surroundings, yet, minimize the negative consequences of a flawed arrest decision process.

In measuring organizational influence over police discretion, it was necessary to isolate those structural, process, and attitudinal characteristics discussed in Chapter 3. Several dimensions of meaning were used to develop the specification of a set of indicators representing the presence or absence of discretionary controls within the organization. These dimensional groupings, placed into four categories for the purpose of this research, are identified as *policy, process, training,* and *values.* For each dimension five specific indicators have been elaborated. Conceptually, each indicator is different from other indicators in that each measures a different aspect of the specified dimension. This is consistent with the statistical notion that indicators should be additive, such that the accumulation of the indicators individually capture different aspects of the dimension and collectively they represent the conceptual space defined by the dimension. The twenty indicators represented in this study capture the different aspects of organizational attempts to influence discretion that are translated into research terms to effectively measure the concept. Using these indicators (predictors) a scale was constructed to measure capacity for organizational influence (control) of police discretion, referred to as the Arrest Discretion Control Scale (ADCS). It is crucial to remember that the issue in measurement of organizational constraints on officer discretion is not the absolute amount of discretion that is permitted. Instead, the focus is upon the extent to which the organization attempts to control the exercise of discretion, where discretion is characterized as the ability of the officer to deviate from department procedures and norms.

A survey instrument was administered to the population of municipal police departments in the United States that contained 200 or more sworn officers on the force. Since the complete population of interest was manageable, a census of the entire population of departments was undertaken rather than a sample. Of the 211 agencies surveyed, 147 (70%) respondents completed and returned the instrument. Data were analyzed utilizing statistical package software (SPSS) to perform multiple regression analysis. Multiple regression has the advantage of giving the independent effect of each variable while controlling for the other variables in the equation. The results of this research conclude that significant associations exist between the Arrest Discretion Control Scale (ADCS) and the variables of organizational size, supervisory levels, number of specialty details, and supervisory span of control. The following section discusses each of the research questions posited in Chapter 1 and their relevance to the study.

Findings and Implications for Current Theory

The first research question in this study examined the observed range of organizational influence on police officer discretion in field arrests among police departments studied. Control of arrest discretion was reflected in four different dimensions that were conceptually separated with different Likert items associated with each dimension. Chapter 3 explains the conceptualization of these dimensions, which include official policy, organizational process, training, and the values structure. Each of these dimensions has specific indicators through which organizational management can attempt to influence or constrain the arrest behavior of officers. Distribution of police departments was done by score along the Arrest Discretion Control Scale (ADCS), a summated ratings scale developed by utilizing the previously identified indicators that make up the four dimensions of discretionary control. Departments ranged in score along the scale from the lowest observed score of 2.90 to the highest score of 5.65. Mean and median scores (4.41 and 4.45 respectively), and the standard deviation (.55) were also calculated for ADCS. Research found substantial variation, relative to the scale dimensions, in how much police departments attempt to control arrest discretion. While scale scores run nearly completely along the six anchor points that are theoretically possible, it becomes apparent that most departments actively attempt to limit or at least delimit officer discretion in making arrests. The majority of departments are concentrated in the scale scores ranging from 3.5 through 5.0. This concentration of law enforcement agencies at the upper end of the ADCS scale tends to illustrate that police departments are concerned with the arrest process and that considerable organizational energy is expended in trying to influence the ways in which street officers handle the activity. Only one department displayed a scale score that is below the midpoint of the scale (3.0), while 78.3% of the departments are at or above the score of 4.0. There was no explicit expectation in terms of distribution of the law enforcement agencies studied and how they would place on the ADCS, however, it was anticipated that the philosophical components of community policing, so widely touted in law enforcement, would have produced organizational structures that supplied officers a broad range of discretion in the arrest decision process, and that those decisions would be influenced more by extralegal considerations and less by legal ones. This study tends to contradict this presumption and raises the question of whether basic organizational structures have not been substantially altered from the conceptions of earlier models that Wilson (1968) defined. However, it is difficult to make comparisons with modern day police agencies to their predecessors since research is mixed. The limited research that has been done with organizational-level variables regarding arrest discretion begs the quest for a better framework of understanding. With the Arrest Discretion Control Scale (ADCS) a baseline for future research can start to develop while helping to enhance our knowledge of how organizational characteristics can be used to manage discretion.

Dimensional Categories

Organizational structures that impact arrest discretion were identified through a review of the research literature. While no two organizations are completely alike, these control structures are essentially embedded in four main areas: official policy, process, training, and values. As stated earlier, these dimensions are used to establish the extent to which the organization attempts to control the exercise of arrest discretion, where discretion is characterized as the ability of the officer to deviate from department procedures and norms. The remainder of this section puts forward the findings of this research for each of the dimensional areas.

Table 16 shows each of the twenty indicators that represent the four dimensions of organizational influence on arrest discretion and displays the number of agencies that responded to that particular indicator, the mean, standard deviation and the lowest and highest score values reported for the 147 departments studied. The extreme of the indicator scores (upper and lower limits) provide additional information for analysis. The upper limit (mean scores ≥ 5.0) indicates that departments provided a significant concurrence with that particular indicator. Three indicators, professional legal review (policy dimension), formal discipline (process dimension), and a field-training program (training dimension) can be found in this range. This tends to indicate that many law enforcement agencies rely heavily on compliance to department rules and training, and are still strongly influenced by legal considerations more than community interests in the arrest decision process.

Table 16. Summary Statistics for Dimensional Predictors

Indicator	N	Min.	Max.	Mean	SD
Specificity of Policy	146	1.00	6.00	5.05	1.16
Professional Legal Review	146	1.00	6.00	5.28	1.02
Shaped Discretion	146	1.00	6.00	4.79	1.25
External Review	146	1.00	6.00	2.92	1.48
Extensiveness of Policy	145	1.00	6.00	4.85	1.23
Face-to-Face Intervention	145	1.00	6.00	3.58	1.68
Case Agent Review	145	1.00	6.00	4.71	1.47
Communication	146	2.00	6.00	4.69	1.05
Discovery	145	1.00	6.00	4.48	1.25
Severity of Sanctions	146	2.00	6.00	5.31	1.00
Field Training Program	147	1.00	6.00	5.43	1.07
Frequency of Training	147	1.00	6.00	4.59	1.20
Supervisor Training	147	1.00	6.00	4.41	1.27
Discretionary Choices	146	1.00	6.00	4.72	.99
Monitoring Effectiveness	147	1.00	6.00	3.95	1.32
Independence	147	1.00	5.00	2.55	1.08
Professionalism	146	1.00	6.00	4.09	1.40
Relationship of Mgmt.	146	1.00	6.00	4.82	1.22
Citizen Review	147	1.00	6.00	3.12	1.83
Community Policing	143	1.00	6.00	4.66	1.28

The lower limit applies to those statement indicators that have a mean scale score below 3.0, and indicates that many agencies did not sense the application of these specific tactics toward organizational control of arrest discretion. There are two statement indicators found in this grouping: external review of written arrest policy (policy dimension) and independence of line officers in the arrest decision process (values system). Interestingly, while it did not fall below 3.0, the department support of citizen review boards for misconduct scored low (mean 3.1) in the values dimension.

Policy Dimension

During this research it was anticipated that the policy dimension would have a significant impact on discretionary control. This is based, in part, on the issue of accountability for law enforcement organizations, the fact that such organizations exist to enforce rule of law, and that policy has long been considered one of the most effective methods in guiding professional police judgment during the reform era of policing. As was expected, the data found in Chapter 4 (See Table 7), shows that most departments that attempt to control arrest discretion place a significant emphasis on policy means. In fact, all of the dimensional areas identified seem to play a significant role in discretion control, albeit, at different degrees. What is surprising is that policy control was not a "standout" as inferred by the literature. Policy and process controls were closely grouped together along mean scores and both had similar rankings in terms of high and low scoring departments. What this means is that law enforcement agencies are relying more on varying aspects of discretion control for arrests than just the "bread and butter" of policy directives. As community policing takes hold in the philosophy of police organizations, police executives are realizing that the expansion of line level discretion must have counterbalances in other areas besides the rule book of do's and don'ts. The highest mean among indicators for policy control was professional legal review of arrest policies (mean 5.28, SD 1.02). A high mean value indicates respondent approval for the use of the content of the item (in this case legal review) as a means of influencing discretion within a department. One explanation for this may be the continued increase in false arrest litigation that many police agencies are experiencing. The lowest mean indicator was the support of external review by citizens groups and politicians (mean 2.92, SD 1.48). Explanations for this can only be surmised at this juncture. It may be that community policing has more inroads to make, or that law enforcement administrators are too concerned that public review of arrest policies would place them in conflict with judiciary precedent.

Process Dimension

The process dimension focused mainly on organizational procedures and protocols such as supervisory review and the disciplinary procedures for intentional violations of arrest policies. As with the other dimensions, the primary focus was to gauge the level of organizational control in arrest discretion. Supervisory review of field arrests (mean 3.58, SD 1.68) was found to have the lowest mean among the process related items, while emphasis on formal discipline for policy violators (mean 5.31, SD 1.00) showed the highest mean score. This is not unexpected given the literature review and the fact that a number of high profile agencies had no supervisory review procedure in place for field arrests until they fell under consent decree (see Chapter 2). Formal discipline measures continue to play a significant role in discretion control, something that has its roots in the beginnings of American law enforcement and the paramilitary structure used to develop police agencies. However, this is disappointing and illustrates the continued reliance on the professional model of policing that focuses on after-the-fact interventions for policy and procedural violations. Police labor groups have long argued that the optimum point of management participation is at the first-line supervisor level, prior to circumstances leading to formal punishment. Even though the research illustrates a strong training foundation among police agencies, it appears that when it relates to management it is in the form of formal discipline as opposed to coaching and mentoring. The line of reasoning is that the ideal intervention point for arrest review should be in the field with the patrol supervisor. At this point the supervisor has the ability to reinforce the officer's decision and provide the foundation for what constitutes a legal and moral arrest or to mentor, coach, and direct the officer in recognized deficiencies of the seizure, thereby limiting negative consequences to the organization, the officer, and the citizen. Such a process meets the professional ethos to develop police officers who understand the tenets of accountability, responsibility, and expertise and their implications for performance and behavior.

Training Dimension
The training dimension items showed a mean score of 4.63. Included in this structure are formalized field training, refresher training for both line personnel and supervisors, discretionary training for specific situations, and evaluations of arrest procedures training. The findings for this dimension are somewhat unexpected due to police executives' complaints that training is one of the most costly and time competitive aspects of law enforcement. In addition, the literature was replete with special interests, labor unions, and media criticism of deficient or missing training programs. This may be more perception than reality.

The item with the highest mean score among training items was the use of a formalized field-training (FTO) program to cover arrest procedures. This indicator had the highest mean score (5.43) of all indicators with a standard deviation of 1.07. Not surprisingly, most agencies rely heavily on their field training to transition officers from the classroom experience to the "real world" application of arrest procedures. Of the 147 agency respondents, 135 (91.8%) stated that they had their own FTO program. The item with the lowest mean in the training dimension addressed evaluations of arrest procedure training, with a mean score of 3.95 and a standard deviation of 1.32. The significant role of training in discretion control may be offset somewhat by the breakdown in review and evaluation of such programs. It should be noted that this research did not attempt to measure student outcomes such as, how much officers learned about the arrest process and how they applied that learning in the field. There is no way to know if student officers were grasping the underlying principles of arrest procedures and policies. Poor training, no matter how well presented, will fail to lead to improved arrest procedures.

Values Dimension

Finally, the values dimension of arrest control involves the perceptions of independence and professionalism of the agency, the relationship of management to line personnel, the allowance of civilian oversight, and the community policing philosophy. Values items had lower overall mean scores than items in any of the other three dimensions. The item with the highest mean among those in the values grouping was the department's position regarding discretion as an excuse for policy violations of arrest procedures (mean 4.82, SD 1.22). This indicates that most agencies do not allow for the recurrent application of "officer discretion" to violate the bounds of arrest protocol. This would seem to coincide with the procedural dimension of formal discipline. The item with the lowest mean addresses the independence of officers to select those criminal laws that they will enforce (mean 2.55, SD 1.08). This may be the most controversial aspect of the survey instrument. Even Davis (1975) reasoned that enforcement of all criminal laws would quickly overburden the criminal justice system and make law enforcement organizations ineffective bureaucracies. Police chiefs are fully aware of the consequences of zero-tolerance programs, and that most of these strategies are temporary and isolated in nature, dealing with a very specific concern. Nonetheless, law enforcement has had its share of critics that argue that the reason for society's laws is to define established standards of conduct and by allowing the street officer to make personal choices in enforcement the fairness of the judicial system is lost. The irony is that a similar number of critics complain that the reform model of policing created professionally remote, internally oriented, legalistic, formalized, and rigid police departments in the efforts to improve integrity and efficiency.

Another item from the values grouping that showed a low mean merits discussion. This indicator involved that of department support for citizen review boards conducting reviews of police misconduct involving arrests. While this indicator was not the lowest in the values dimension it placed behind only independence (mean 2.55) and external review of arrest policies (mean 2.92) with a displayed mean score of 3.12 and a standard deviation of 1.83. This becomes significant as law enforcement executives strive to move toward community policing strategies of open and cooperative policing. A major precept of community policing is the expectation that officers will be more selective in making arrests and that those decisions will be influenced more by extralegal considerations and less by legal ones. Without citizen participation these extralegal considerations are left to the interpretation of police management, which prior to this point had such decisions made for them through legal directives, although some argument can be made for the manipulation and interpretation of law. It would seem obvious that citizen participation in the review of arrest procedures and police conduct would be a powerful combination in the development of the professional ethos of any law enforcement organization, one that could pay tremendous dividends down the road.

It was acknowledged in Chapter 3 that measuring the police culture is no easy task. The presumption was that police agencies with high levels of discretionary control would incorporate a rigorous value system into their culture. With the advent of community policing it is believed that the police culture and value system becomes even more significant in terms of arrest discretion control. It was somewhat disappointing to find the values structure at the low end of the dimensional scales while prominent scholars (Goldstein, 1990; Kelling, 1999; Walker, 1993) have advocated the importance of the principles of responsibility and accountability to be ingrained into the culture of policing. This research tends to indicate that police administrators must do more to instill a value system that promotes the practice of legal and ethical arrests.

Research Questions With Significant Association

The thrust of this research is driven by the hypotheses developed and discussed in Chapter 1. These propositions were created and developed to test the relationship between certain variables.   Sometimes hypotheses establish a clear and convincing relationship, other times they do not. The objective of this section is to elaborate first on those research questions that displayed a significant level of association to the dependent variable. Next, those research hypotheses that failed to show significance are discussed.

The independent variables identified for this study deal with characteristics of the police department and are internal to the organization. For purposes of this research they include the following: 1) how bureaucratic the police agency is, 2) the level of professionalism of the department, 3) the size of the police department, and 4) supervision levels (span of control).

Number of Sworn Personnel

Department size can be measured in a variety of ways, however, for purposes of this research size relates to the number of sworn police officers in the agency. In Chapter 3 it was postulated that the measure of size would be inversely correlated with an agency's discretion control. In other words, as the number of sworn personnel increases for a department, their score on the Arrest Discretion Control Scale (ADCS) would decrease. The data confirm this expectation, with the number of sworn personnel generating a statistically significant beta value of -.31 (P<.01). The regression analysis presents this correlate as the strongest statistically significant predictor of the ADCS scale. The implication is that as a department gets larger it will suffer deterioration in the management of arrest discretion control. This would tend to support the theory that small police departments may be easier to control by supervisors and that discretion in large agencies is less accountable. Nevertheless, it appears that the research establishes that large police departments have less effective controls on their members, less group stability, and fewer and less effective arrest discretion controls. It is necessary to point out that one of the limitations of this research included surveying only those agencies that contained 200 or more sworn officers on the department. By comparison, most law enforcement agencies across the United States are made up of agencies less than 200 officers. It is unknown how these agencies would compare in similar research and what the threshold for impact would be to smaller police departments (e.g., agencies from 10 to 50 officers see no appreciable difference in the ADCS). Interestingly, as size seems to have the most significant correlation to arrest discretion control the irony is that many police chiefs are convinced that they are understaffed and are always looking for ways to increase their sworn staffing.

Supervisory Span of Control

Another research question asks, what is the relationship between supervisory span of control and the organizational influence of police officer discretion in field arrests? For purposes of this research span of control refers to the structure in the number of employees to first line supervisors in the field. A wide span of control exists when a supervisor oversees many subordinates; a narrow span of control exists when a manager oversees few subordinates.

The belief is that a low ratio of officers to supervisor would have elevated influence and control over police discretionary choices in field arrests. One obvious way a supervisor has of influencing discretion and maintaining some control over patrol officers is simply by being present at the scene of a call. Those agencies that have a high number of officers for each supervisor are expected to have less effective controls on their members, and in today's litigious society, with the risk of discipline involved in improper arrests, those officers are more likely to avoid arrest situations if not effectively supervised. The principle of "span of control" was initially adopted from psychologists, and this principle has been applied to military and administrative operations. Whereas some researchers have suggested the optimal number of workers for any task is between five and seven (Bass, 1960; Indik, 1965), it has generally been accepted that this ideal rarely applied itself to police work, and that most law enforcement agencies operated at a substantially higher ratio.

The majority of police agencies examined (79%) identified their officer to supervisor ratio at six to nine patrol officers for each supervisor. This finding was somewhat unexpected since it was at the middle to lower end of the categorical selections. Since police departments that have 200 or more officers are considered in the medium to high range it was anticipated that the officer to supervisor ratio would be at the higher end of the spectrum (e.g., 10-12 officers per supervisor). The literature has been critical of the tendency in modern police operations to exceed the bounds of effective control, whether due to manpower limitations, cost, or motorized policing (Iannone, 1980). In Chapter 3 it was hypothesized that supervisor span of control would be positively related to department levels of influence over arrest discretion. Those police departments that have a high ratio of officers for each supervisor were expected to have less effective controls on their members. This correlate generated a beta of -.17, indicating that as the number of officers assigned to one supervisor increases, the department score on the influencing arrest discretion scale decreases. Supervisor span of control, as expected, had a positive relation to department levels of influence over arrest discretion.

The issue of increased levels of control with low officer to supervisor ratios may seem apparent to police administrators, however, research in the calculation of span of control formulas has been essentially non-existent in police work. Meier and Bohte (2003) argue that research on span of control has virtually disappeared from the scholarly scene, but that practitioners remain very curious about the impacts on the workplace.

Findings That Fail to Support Hypotheses

The following research question was asked regarding bureaucracy. What is the relationship between bureaucracy and the organizational influence on police discretion in field arrests?

It was expected that departments with a high degree of bureaucratization become focused on a "conception of order" meaning a strict compliance with rules and regulations, therefore, it was postulated that the higher the bureaucratic composition of a police department the more significant will be the organizational influence over discretionary decision making regarding field arrests.

Two indicators were used to operationalize bureaucracy, one being rank structure and the other work divisions within the department. As the number of work divisions increased within the organization there was a negative correlation to the ADCS scale. In Chapter 4 it was determined that the beta coefficient had a negative correlation (-.13) but was not large enough to be statistically reliable (p>.05). The second indicator, the number of command levels, was statistically significant when compared to the ADCS (beta = .25, p<.01). It was determined that the relationship between bureaucracy and arrest discretion control did not support the stated hypothesis. It was pointed out in Chapter 3 that bureaucracy was based on rather eclectic elements of the literature and that operationalizations of the term have varied significantly in previous research. This makes it extremely difficult to make assessments that apply themselves in a comprehensive manner. Future research would do well to elaborate a more common underpinning for comparisons with such organizational-level variables.

Professionalism

The next research question involves the relationship between organizational professionalism and the influence on police officer discretion in field arrests. Past studies have produced varied and conflicting results (Smith and Klein, 1983) regarding the operationalization of professionalism and how it impacts the arrest process. As with bureaucracy, the correlate of professionalism combines two indicators for purposes of this research. Professionalism is represented by the amount of entry level education required for new police officers and the number of specialty units that are staffed by the agency. For purposes of this research, professionalism is designed to illustrate the organization's amount of autonomy given to a position that displays a high level of education, experience, and skill in the field of policing. Because it was anticipated that such autonomy would provide a higher level of discretion for the officer it was expected that the level of professionalism in a department would be inversely related to the level of attempted influence on arrest discretion. The number of specialty details found in police departments did, in fact, show a statistically significant influence over the ADCS. However, this was a positive correlation to increases in the ADCS score, which is contrary to the hypothesis presented in Chapter 3. One reason for this may be a difference in expectations in the patrol function from that of a specialty position. Greater flexibility may be provided for officers that have displayed the requisite skill to make sound decisions in the field, therefore, providing them the opportunity to work in a specialty detail.

The presence of educational requirements is also positively related to the Arrest Discretion Control Scale, with a beta of .14, but this value is not statistically significant (p>.05). As mentioned in Chapter 4, the relatively low correlation of education might be a function of the lack of variation among police departments on the entry-level educational requirement. More than 70 percent of the departments are in the same category (HS/GED), and there is little variation on this variable that is available to explain variation in the arrest discretion control scale. Many police scholars have argued the need for higher standards in educational requirements but practitioners are resistant to increasing such requirements due to the limited applicant pool. As can be seen in Chapter 4, less than 20 percent of respondent agencies require any type of college degree as an entrance requirement. Care should be given in interpreting these results since they do not capture the level of education after an officer is employed. Many agencies provide educational assistance, and may even have educational requirements for promotion or transfer. The scope of this research did not allow for the complexity of gathering this information from respondent agencies, though this could be an important topic area for future research.

Limitations of the Study
The research population for this study was limited to municipal law enforcement agencies in the United States with 200 or more sworn police officers. Smaller agencies, county and state departments, and those law enforcement agencies outside the United States are not considered. The results of this research are not analogous to groups outside the research study, although, inferences may be drawn from this study for the purpose of framing research questions that include groups outside the test subjects.

In addition, this research relies on the perceptions of law enforcement administrators about the structures of their agency. The study makes no judgment regarding the quality of such structures, but instead measures the impact that these structures have on arrest discretion management. While research in the area of police discretion is limited, and has only recently come to the forefront, there is much to be learned about the cause and effect factors. There are but four factors being measured in their applicability to the problem at hand in this research. This creates questions as to the pertinence of such organizational variables and the missing elements that may play a more vital role in police discretion. The theoretical component involving police discretion at the organizational level is associated with a variety of frameworks that fails to provide a single construct for analysis. The operationalization of police discretion in this study may not correlate well to future research. However, it is believed that such examination is instrumental in establishing foci for future research and will help to lay the groundwork for such studies.

Implications for Professional Practitioners

Regarding the dimensions of *policy* and *process*, the trend toward controlling the actions of police officers through formal rules continues to be a highly utilized and legitimate method when dealing with the management of arrest discretion. But administrative rulemaking should not be relied upon as the sole approach to controlling discretionary choices. Walker (1993) makes the argument that formal rules designed to control discretion tend to collapse over time into what he refers to as "empty formalism." Essentially, Walker was alluding to police officers going through the motions of compliance and finding ways to get around the formal process; for example, misrepresenting the facts surrounding probable cause or reading Miranda warnings and then attempting to extract confessions regardless of the suspect's response. Believing that policies are purely symbolic and are designed primarily to placate interest groups leans heavily to the cynical view of rulemaking. This research verifies that police departments continue to depend heavily on formalized policy and procedures to guide and manage arrest discretion. However, the research raises some question about whether such policies are effectively communicated to rank and file officers. It also points to the aversion of a significant number of police agencies studied to involve the community in the rulemaking process.

The literature illustrates that administrative rules have been very effective in limiting police shooting discretion (see Chapter 2) with positive results in terms of social policy. This shows that officers do appear to comply with rules, and that these rules can provide a significant contribution in discretion control efforts. Nevertheless, police practitioners should not rely on formal rules alone to guide arrest discretion, but instead look at discretion management in a multi-faceted context of control mechanisms.

On the topic of *training*, most agencies rely heavily on their field training programs to provide comprehensive arrest procedures training, however, this research did not measure the effectiveness of such training. It is important to point out that many scholars make a case that teaching "discretionary choices" should be done in the classroom, more preferably in scenario based training, long before the officer is forced to make decisions that they are ill prepared for. The training dimension illustrated that a significant number of agencies failed to adequately monitor the effectiveness of their arrest procedures training for line personnel and first-line supervisors. This is a critical element of training since an effective assessment can lead to better training techniques and feedback for management in the design of future training programs.

As police agencies continue to work on developing relationships with the community, police executives need to find ways to guide discretion and police behavior generally through increasing reliance on *values* instead of relying strictly on rules and protocols of accountability. Lipsky (1980) reasoned that street-level bureaucrats (i.e., police officers) have tremendous discretion when dealing with the public at large. These decisions, many times, are made on the basis of the bureaucrats' own ethical underpinnings. Davis (1969) goes on to point out that, "discretion is a tool, indispensable for individualization of justice." This leads to the point that no combination of mechanisms for enforcing administrative responsibility can remove the element of judgment from police officers. Law enforcement administrators have a management responsibility to create a "corporate" culture of accountability and responsibility for their line officers. This culture is defined by the methods, procedures, and forces that determine what values will be reflected in arrest discretion decisions. This is no easy task, especially when trying to balance competing interests, values, and interpretations of fact. It also requires the involvement of the community in the rule making and review processes of the law enforcement agency. This is one area that the research found in which police executives displayed a weak showing.

In terms of organizational characteristics most police executives may find that they have limited influence, at least initially, over the configuration of their department size, supervisory span of control, and the division and rank structure of the agency. Yet, these variables are significantly related to the ability of the organization to mitigate unnecessary discretion in the arrest decision process. Even necessary discretion must be properly confined, structured, and checked. By knowing how these department structures affect arrest discretion, police managers can develop their strategic plans to take advantage of the potential benefits of these characteristics in providing a more professional and constitutionally valid law enforcement organization.

Recommendations for Further Research

The problems of poor quality arrests encompass a variety of topics and training challenges. This research looks at these issues as being systemic in nature requiring a unified approach to change them. One of the best recommendations is a clear and consistent communication of expectations for appropriate arrest behavior. This "Best Practices" approach requires further research in analyzing those organizational-level variables that impact the management of arrest discretion. The baseline has been provided in the conceptual dimensions of arrest discretion control, however, additional research to further test the validity of these predictors will help to gain a greater understanding of the science of the field, and to serve law enforcement administrators in establishing a higher level of professionalism in the field. A way to accomplish this task is the use of different methodologies in constructing a measurable scale for discretion control. One recommendation is that of factor analysis, which is a technique used to investigate the relationship between theoretical concepts and empirical indicators (Babbie, 1998). It is used to reduce a large number of items to a smaller, more manageable number of indices. The benefit is in using a small number of independent variables known as factors (supervariables) to explain a lot of the variance in the dependent variable of interest. This technique can be helpful in showing which items should be used in an index and how they should be weighed. Factor analysis is based on complex statistics, but is widely used across the social sciences in building reliable, compact scales for measuring social and psychological variables.

Further research needs to determine whether similar associations of arrest discretion control are found in different populations of law enforcement agencies. Only those municipal police departments with 200 or more sworn officers were identified for the purposes of this research. There are more than 18,000 local, county, state, and federal law enforcement agencies in the United States and many of those agencies have well under 200 officers in their employment. Since officer size was found to have a significant association in the amount of discretion control it seems only prudent that agencies outside the study population should be given consideration in future research.

The literature reveals that almost no research has addressed how organizations determine spans of control or what difference it makes. This is another variable that displayed a significant association with arrest discretion control. Interestingly, of the top 20 agencies that scored a 5.0 or higher on the Arrest Discretion Control Scale, 16 (80%) of those police departments had spans of control of nine officers or fewer. It is not the intent of this research to provide a prescription for supervisory capacity in terms of field officers, but it is important to illustrate the role that first-line supervisors have in the management of arrest discretion. In addition, the implication of these findings is not meant to suggest that span of control can be viewed as a model for varying levels within an organization. The influence of span of control relationships at the lower levels of supervision found in this research may be, and probably are, totally irrelevant to how spans of control are structured at higher levels in these organizations. By finding the proper balance in supervisory oversight in the field, agencies may effectively enhance their arrest discretion control, thereby, reducing false arrest litigation and civil rights claims. This should be an important area for future research.

Finally, further research needs to be done in the area of education and its relationship to arrest discretion management. The findings in Chapter 4 found educational entrance requirements positively related to the ADCS scores, but with a beta of .14 this value was not statistically significant ($p > .05$). It was determined that the relatively low correlation of education might be a function of the lack of variation among departments on the entry-level educational requirement. More than 70 percent of the departments studied were in the same category for educational requirements. It is possible that a different sample wherein departments had more varied entrance requirements would show a higher magnitude of correlation. In addition, future research needs to examine the relationship of education after hire. Many agencies provide for tuition assistance or incentive programs to pursue higher academic degrees after certain time periods of employment. The effects of these types of programs and their impact on arrest discretion control provide possibilities for further research.

Conclusions

The focus of this research has been the influence of organizational characteristics on street-level discretion (decision-making) by police officers in making field arrests. Conceptually, organizational influence on police officer discretion is multi-faceted. That is, different aspects of organizational characteristics and processes combine to create a particular level of organizational constraint or influence on officer arrest discretion. Because there has been considerable research focus placed on individual, situational, and even community level indicators regarding police discretionary behavior, the unit of analysis for this study has been the organization. The objective of the research was to seek explanations and predictions that will generalize to similar organizations.

Law enforcement executives have a fundamental responsibility in assuring that their police officers know how to properly execute the arrest process without violating the rights of community residents. This knowledge base comes from a versatile set of dimensions that include formal policy, department procedures, training, and a value system ingrained into the professional ethos. Arrest issues are no less critical to policing than those that pertained to the use of deadly force thirty years ago. Laws, policies, and standards related to arrest procedures are constantly in flux, thereby requiring constant re-education and training in the practice of legal and ethical arrest decisions. As detailed previously, a comparatively small number of arrests in this country results in any appreciable prosecution, and an even smaller number results in conviction. However, police agencies maintain that one of their primary objectives is supporting the prosecution of criminals. The arrest decision process has represented a major gap when placed in the conceptual area of discretion control. This gives researchers and administrators substantial reason to begin to think about those factors that impact the critical arrest decision, especially in the area of the organizational level of scrutiny, which has been gravely lacking. This study provides empirical research in the area of organizational structures that helps to close this gap.

APPENDIX
RESEARCH QUESTIONNAIRE

POLICE DEPARTMENT SURVEY

Please provide the following information on the primary person who is completing this questionnaire. In addition, you will find questions that provide demographic and procedural information about your organization. The information you provide is for statistical purposes only and will remain **completely confidential**.

1. Name of your department:

2. Name:	Assignment or Title:
Rank:	Years of Service:	Work Phone:
Fax:		E-Mail:

Please mark an X in the box that most accurately describes your department.

3. Number of sworn personnel in your department.

☐ Fewer than 300   ☐ 301-500   ☐ 501-1000   ☐ 1001-1500

☐ 1501-2000   ☐ 2001-3000   ☐ More than 3000

4. Please check the number of levels of police <u>supervision</u> in your department. For example, a department with officers, sergeants, a commander and the chief would have **3** levels of police supervision. Officers would not count as a level of supervision.

☐ 2 levels or fewer   ☐ 3 levels   ☐ 4 levels

☐ 5 levels   ☐ 6 levels   ☐ 7 or more levels

5. Check the number of work divisions within your department. For example: the patrol division (you may have more than one), investigations division, management services division, legal support division, community relations division, etc.

☐ None   ☐ 1-2   ☐ 3-4   ☐ 5-6   ☐ 7-8   ☐ 9 or more divisions

141

6.   Place a check next to each of the specialty assignments below that
     currently exist in your department.

☐ *Public*   ☐ *Bicycle Detail*   ☐ *Community*
Affairs/Media   *Relations*

☐ *Air Support*   ☐ *SWAT*   ☐ *Mounted*
                                               Unit
☐ *K-9 Detail*   ☐ *Motorcycle*   ☐ *School*
                      officers   *Resource*

☐ *DARE*   ☐ *Planning &*   ☐ *FTO*
                      Research

7.   What is the <u>*average*</u> number of patrol officers assigned to one street
     supervisor?

☐ *5 or fewer*   ☐ *6-7*   ☐ *8-9*

☐ *10-11*   ☐ *12-13*   ☐ *14 or more*

8.   Please check the amount of <u>*entry-level*</u> education required to become
     a police officer with your department.

☐ *None*   ☐ *High School*   ☐ *Some*
                      or GED   *College*
☐ *2yr College*   ☐ *4yr Degree*   ☐ *Above 4yr*
Degree   *Degree*

9.   Check the <u>*maximum*</u> amount of educational assistance provided or
     offered to officers of your department during the fiscal year.

☐ *None*   ☐ *$1-500*   ☐ *$501-1000*

☐ *$1001-2000*   ☐ *$2001-3000*   ☐ *$3001 or*
                                               More

Please consider the statements below as they relate to your police department.
Indicate the extent of agreement or disagreement by circling the appropriate
response (SA = Strongly Agree, A = Agree, SWA = Somewhat Agree, SWD =
Somewhat Disagree, D = Disagree, and SD = Strongly Disagree).

	SA	*A*	*SWA*	*SWD*	*D*	*SD*
10. Department arrest policy is **very specific** and defines the basic elements necessary to constitute an arrest (i.e., intent, authority, seizure, and understanding).	*SA*	*A*	*SWA*	*SWD*	*D*	*SD*
11. This department **promotes** the use of professional legal review of written arrest policies prior to implementation.	*SA*	*A*	*SWA*	*SWD*	*D*	*SD*
12. Department arrest policy gives **clear** guidance for the decision to arrest in specific situations for specific crimes.	*SA*	*A*	*SWA*	*SWD*	*D*	*SD*
13. This department **strongly supports** external review (e.g., citizen panels, town hall, city council, etc.) of arrest policies prior to implementation.	*SA*	*A*	*SWA*	*SWD*	*D*	*SD*
14. This department has **extensive** written policies governing the procedures for arrest.	*SA*	*A*	*SWA*	*SWD*	*D*	*SD*
15. A patrol supervisor **routinely** reviews and approves field arrests prior to booking.	*SA*	*A*	*SWA*	*SWD*	*D*	*SD*

16.	A supervisor or detective **routinely** reviews criminal field arrest reports prior to the suspect's preliminary (probable cause) hearing.	SA	A	SWA	SWD	D	SD
17.	This department **frequently** utilizes effective communications methods to make known to officers recurrent problems with arrests.	SA	A	SWA	SWD	D	SD
18.	This department has **organizational mechanisms** in place to detect **all** but very minor violations of arrest procedures.	SA	A	SWA	SWD	D	SD
19.	This department places **strong emphasis** on formal discipline for any officer that intentionally violates arrest procedures.	SA	A	SWA	SWD	D	SD
20.	This department has a formalized field training process (FTO) that **comprehensively** covers arrest procedures.	SA	A	SWA	SWD	D	SD
21.	Patrol officers **frequently** receive formal refresher training in arrest procedures.	SA	A	SWA	SWD	D	SD
22.	Patrol supervisors **frequently** receive formal refresher training in arrest procedures.	SA	A	SWA	SWD	D	SD

23. Department training
    specifically addresses *the*   SA   A   SWA   SWD   D   SD
    use of officer discretion in
    the decision to arrest

24. *This department*
    consistently *uses formal*
    evaluations of arrest   SA   A   SWA   SWD   D   SD
    procedure training to
    improve the quality of such
    training.

25. *It is* **acknowledged** *that*
    officers will sometimes
    make arrest decisions on   SA   A   SWA   SWD   D   SD
    criteria not covered by
    written policy or standard
    procedure.

26. *Officers are expected to*
    enforce **all** *criminal laws*   SA   A   SWA   SWD   D   SD
    within the bounds of full
    enforcement.

27. *This department* **regularly**
    allows *for the use of*
    discretion to be an excuse   SA   A   SWA   SWD   D   SD
    for policy violations of
    arrest procedures.

28. *This department* **supports**
    the use of a review board
    that includes citizens to   SA   A   SWA   SWD   D   SD
    conduct reviews of serious
    police misconduct
    involving arrests.

29. *This department* **promotes**
    community-policing
    interests over   SA   A   SWA   SWD   D   SD
    considerations of
    individual rights in arrest
    situations.

30. On the continuum below, <u>circle the number</u> that most accurately
describes the way your department functions on a day-to-day basis.
The boxes below the continuum give examples of the two extreme
positions and the center-point.

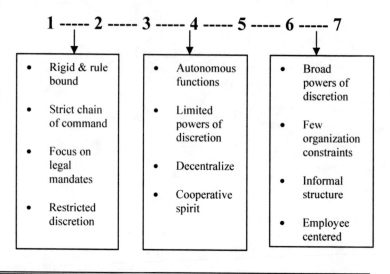

1 ----- 2 ----- 3 ----- 4 ----- 5 ----- 6 ----- 7

Rigid & rule bound	Autonomous functions	Broad powers of discretion

- Rigid & rule bound
- Strict chain of command
- Focus on legal mandates
- Restricted discretion

- Autonomous functions
- Limited powers of discretion
- Decentralize
- Cooperative spirit

- Broad powers of discretion
- Few organization constraints
- Informal structure
- Employee centered

Thank you for your participation in this important research!

*For those agencies that would like a copy of the research summary to
this study please check the box below:*
    ❑   *Yes, please send a copy of the research summary*

Please return this questionnaire by fax to:
Commander Richard Groeneveld, (602) 495-3660
Otherwise, please use the postage-paid, pre-addressed envelope.

REFERENCES

Altheide, D. L. (1996). *Qualitative media analysis.* Thousand Oaks, CA: Sage University.

Andrews, A. H. Jr. (1985). Structuring the political independence of the police chief. In W. A. Geller (Ed.), *Police Leadership in America: Crisis and Opportunity* (pp. 5-19). New York, NY: Praeger.

Babbie, E. (1998). *The practice of social research.* Belmont, CA: Wadsworth Publishing Company.

Bass, B. M. (1960). *Leadership, psychology, and organizational behavior.* New York, NY: Harper.

Barker, T. (1978). An empirical study of police deviance other than corruption. *Journal of Police Science and Administration, 6,* 3, 264-272.

Bayley, D. H. & Mendelsohn, H. (1969). *Minorities and the police: Confrontation in America.* New York, NY: Free Press.

Bertalanffy, L. V. (1968). *General system theory: Foundations, development,applications.* New York, NY: George Braziller.

Bittner, E. (1970). *The functions of police in modern society.* Rockville, MD: National Institute of Mental Health.

Blalock, H. (1964). *Causal inferences in nonexperimental research.* Chapel Hill, NC:University of North Carolina Press.

Blalock, H. (1982). *Conceptualization and measurement in the social sciences.* Thousand Oaks, CA: Sage Publications.

Bopp, W. J. (1984). *Crises in police administration.* Springfield, IL: Charles C. Thomas.

Boyle, R.P. (1970). Path analysis and ordinal data. *American Journal of Sociology, January, 75,* 461-480.

Brown, M. K. (1988). *Working the street: Police discretion and the dilemmas of reform.* New York, NY: Russell Sage Foundation.

Byrne, D. (1999). *Complexity theory and the social sciences: An introduction.* New York, NY: Routledge.

Cannon, L. (1997). *Official negligence: How Rodney King and the riots changed Los Angeles and the LAPD.* New York: NY. Times Books.

Carte, G. E. (1975). *Police reform in the United States: The era of August Vollmer.* Berkeley, CA: University of California Press.

Child, J. (1973). Predicting and understanding organization structure. *Administrative Science Quarterly, 18,* 168-185.

City of Canton v. Harris, 489 U. S. 378, 396 (1989).

Conkrite, C. L. (1983). Facing increased crime with decreasing resources. *FBI Law Bulletin, 52,* 4.

Crank, J. P. (1990). The influence of environmental and organizational factors on police style in urban and rural environments. *Journal of Research in Crime and Delinquency, 27,* 166-189.

Dahl, R. A. (1982). *Dilemmas of pluralistic democracy: Autonomy vs. control.* Binghampton, NY: Yale University Press.

Davis, K. C. (1968). *Discretionary justice: A preliminary inquiry.* Westport, CN: Greenwood Press.

Davis, K. C. (1975). *Police discretion.* St. Paul, MN: West Publishing Co.

DeParis, R. J. (2000). How contemporary police agencies can adapt to the community policing mission. *Police Chief, 67,* 8, 108-114.

Dillman, D. A. (1978). *Mail and telephone surveys: the total design method.* New York, NY: Wiley-Interscience Publishing.

Dodenhoff, P. (1985). Interview: Robert Kliesmet. *Law Enforcement News, January, 21,* 9-11.

Dugan, J. R. & Breda, D. R. (1991). Complaints about police officers: A comparison among types and agencies. *Journal of Criminal Justice, 19, 2,* 165-171.

Duncan, O. D. (1975). *Structural equation models.* New York, NY: Academic Press.

Edwards, A. L. (1957). *Techniques of attitude scale construction.* New York, NY: Appleton-Century-Crofts Publishing.

Emery, F. E. ed. (1969). *Systems thinking: Selected readings.* Baltimore, MD: Penguin Books.

Ericson, R. (1982). *Reproducing order: A study of police patrol work.* Toronto: University of Toronto Press.

Federal Bureau of Investigation (1997). *Civil rights program.* Seminar class presented at the FBI National Academy. Quantico, VA.

Federal Bureau of Investigation (2003). *Uniform Crime Reports.* Washington, DC: Department of Justice.

Felkenes, G. T. (1993). *The impact of Fanchon Blake v. City of Los Angeles.* Claremont, CA: Claremont Graduate School. In J. H. Skolnick & J. J. Fyfe, *Above The Law: Police and the Excessive Use of Force.* New York, NY: The Free Press.

Fox, R.J., M. R. Crask, and J. Kim, (1988). Mail survey response rate. *Public Opinion Quarterly 52,* 467-91.

Frederickson, H. G. (1997). *The spirit of public administration.* San Francisco, CA: Jossey-Bass Inc.

Gouldner, Alvin, (1954). *Patterns of industrial bureaucracy.* New York: Free Press.

Goldstein, H. (1977). *Policing a free society.* Cambridge, MA: Ballinger Publishing Co.

Goldstein, H. (1986). Administrative problems in controlling the exercise of police authority. In M. R. Pogrebin & R. M. Regoli (Eds.), *Police Administrative Issues: Techniques and Functions.* New York, NY: Associated Faculty Press.

Goldstein, H. (1990). *Problem oriented policing.* New York: NY. McGraw-Hill, Inc.

Goldstein, H. (2000). Improving policing: A problem-oriented approach. In W. M. Oliver (Ed.), *Community Policing: Classical Readings.* Upper Saddle River, NJ: Prentice-Hall.

Graham v. Connor, 490 U.S. 386 (1989).

Hall, J. (1999). Due process and deadly force: When police conduct shocks the conscience. *FBI Law Bulletin, 68,* 2, p. 27.

Heise, D. R. (1975). *Causal analysis.* New York, NY: John Wiley and Sons.

Henerson, M. E., Morris, L. L., and Fitz-Gibbon, C. T. (1987). *How to measure attitudes.* Newbury Park, CA: Sage Publications.

Horton, R. D. (1970). Municipal labor relations in New York. *Proceedings of the Academy of Political Science, 68.*

Horton, R. (1985). *The general linear model.* New York, NY: Seminar Press.

Iannone, N. F. (1980). *Supervision of police personnel.* Englewood Cliffs, N.J: Prentice-Hall

Independent Commission on the Los Angeles Police Department (1991). *Report of the Independent Commission of the Los Angeles Police Department.*

Indik, B. P. (1965). Organizational size and member participation: Some empirical tests of alternative explanations. *Human Relations, 18,* 339-350.

Kaplan, Abraham, 1964. *The conduct of inquiry.* San Francisco, CA: Chandler Publishers.

Kast, F. E. & Rosenzweig, J. E. (1972). General systems theory: Applications for organization and management. *Academy of Management Journal, 12,* 447.

Katz, D. & Kahn, R. L. (1992). Oranizations and the system concept. In J. M. Shafritz & C. Hyde (Eds.), *Classics of Public Adminstration* (pp 248-259). 3rd Ed. Pacific Grove, CA: Brooks/Cole Publishing Co.

Kaufman, H. (1969). Bureaucrats and organized civil servants. *Proceedings of the Academy of Political Science,* 41.

Kelling, G. (1999). Broken windows and police discretion. *National Institute of Justice Research Report (NCJ 178259).* U.S. Department of Justice.

Kelling, G. L., Wasserman, R., & Williams, H. (2000). Police accountability and community policing. In W. M. Oliver (Ed.), *Community Policing: Classical Readings* (pp. 269-279). Upper Saddle River, NJ: Prentice Hall.

Kelly, M. J. (1975). *Police chief selection: A handbook for local government.* Washington D.C.: Police Foundation.

Kelner, J. & Munves, J. (1980). *The Kent State coverup.* New York, NY: Harper & Row.

Kerstetter, W. A. (1985). Who disciplines the police? Who should? In W. A. Geller (Ed.), *Police Leadership in America: Crisis and Opportunity* (pp. 149-183). New York, NY: Praeger.

Kingdon, J. W. (1984). *Agendas, alternatives, and public policies.* Boston, MA: Little, Brown and Company.

Klockars, C. B. (1985). *The idea of police.* Beverly Hills, CA: Sage Publications.

Knoke, D. and Bohrnstedt, G. W. (1994). *Statistics for social data analysis.* Itasca, IL: F.E. Peacock Publishers.

LaFave, W. R. (1965). *Arrest: The decision to take a suspect into custody.* Boston, MA: Little Brown.

Lewis-Beck, M. (1980). *Applied regression analysis.* Beverly Hills, CA: Sage Publications.

Lipsky, M. (1980). *Street-level bureaucracy: Dilemmas of the individual in public services.* New York, NY: Russell Sage Foundation.

Leonard, V. A. & More, H. W. (2000). *Police organization and management.* New York, NY: Foundation Press.

Lohman, J. D. & Misner, G. E. (1966). The police and the community: The dynamics of their relationship in a changing society. *President's Commission on Law Enforcement and Administration of Justice.* Washington, DC: U.S. Government Printing Office.

Manning, P. K. (1980). Violence and the police role. *Annals of the American Academy of Political and Social Science, 452,* 135-144.

Manning, P. (1997). *Police work: The social organization of policing.* 2nd Ed. Prospect Heights, IL: Waveland Press.

Mastrofski, S. D. (1981). Policing the beat: The impact of organizational scale on patrol officer behavior in urban residential neighborhoods. *Journal of Criminal Justice 9,* 343-358.

Mastrofski, S. D., Ritti, R., and Hoffmaster, D. (1987). Organizational determinants of police discretion: The case of drinking –driving. *Journal of Criminal Justice 15,* 387-402.

Matlack, W. F. (1993). *Statistics for public managers.* Itasca, IL: F.E. Peacock Publishers.

McLaughlin, V. (1992). *Police and the use of force.* Westport, CT: Praeger Publishers.

Meier, K. J., & Bohte, J. (2003). Span of control and public organizations: Implementing Luther Gulick's research design. *Public Administration Review, 63,* 1, 61-70.

Miranda v. State of Arizona, 384 U. S. 436 (1966)

Monell v. Department of Social Services of the City of New York et al., 436 U.S. 658 (1978).

Monroe v. Pape, 365 U. S. 167 (1961)

Morrison, D. F. (1976). *Multivariate statistical methods.* New York, NY: McGraw-Hill Book Company.

Mosteller, F. and Tukey, J. W. (1977). *Data analysis and regression.* Reading, MA: Addison-Wesley Publishers.

Mueller, J., Schussler, K. and Costner, H. (1977). *Statistical reasoning in sociology.* New York, NY: Houghton-Mifflin.

Muir, W. K. Jr. (1977). *Police: streetcorner politicians.* Chicago, IL: University of Chicago Press.

Munro, J. L. (1974). *Administrative behavior and police organization.* Cincinnati, OH: W. H. Anderson Co.

Munro, J. L. (1979). A general systems strategy for the analysis of criminal justice policy. In F. A. Meyer & R. Baker (Eds.), *Determinants of Law-Enforcement Policies* (pp. 3-13). Lexington, MA: Lexington Books.

Murphy, P. V. and Pate, T. (1977). *Commissioner.* New York, NY: Simon and Shuster.

National Directory of Law Enforcement Administrators, Correctional Institutions, and Related Agencies (1999). *The National Public Safety Information Bureau.* Stevens Point, WI: Span Publishing, Inc.

Neter, J., Wasserman, W. & Kutner, M. (1985). *Applied statistical models.* Homewood, IL: Irwin Publishers.

Niederhoffer, A. (1976). *The ambivalent force: Perspectives on the police.* Chicago, IL: Dryden Press.

Pate, A. M. & Fridell, L. A. (1993). *Police use of force: Official reports, citizen complaints, and legal consequences.* Washington, DC: Police Foundation.

Petersilia, J., Abrahamse, A., and Wilson, J. (1987). *Police performance and case attrition.* Santa Monica, CA: Rand Corporation.

Pogrebin, M. R., & Regoli, R. M. (Eds.). (1986). *Police administrative issues: Techniques and functions.* Millwood, NY: Associated Faculty Press, Inc.

Porter, B. D. (1984). *The Miami riot of 1980: crossing the bounds.* Lexington, MA: Lexington Books.

President's Commission on Law Enforcement and Administration of Justice (1967). *Task Force Report: The Police.* Washington, DC: U.S. Government Printing Office.

Rampart Area Corruption Incident (2000). *Report of the Los Angeles Police Department Board of Inquiry.* Public Report.

Reiss, A. J. Jr. (1985). Shaping and serving the community: The role of the police chief executive. In W. A. Geller (Ed.), *Police leadership in America: Crisis and opportunity* (pp. 61-69). New York, NY: Praeger.

Reynolds, E. A. (1998). *Before the bobbies: The night watch and police reform in metropolitan London, 1720-1830.* Basingstoke, Hampshire: Macmillan.

Riksheim, E. C., and Chermak, S. M. (1993). Causes of police behavior revisited. *Journal of Criminal Justice 21,* 353-382.

Robbins, S. P. (1976). *The administrative process; integrating theory and practice.* Englewood Cliffs, NJ: Prentice-Hall.

Rubinstein, J. (1973). *City police.* New York, NY: Garrar, Straus & Giroux.

Scott, W. G. (1996). Organization theory, an overview and appraisal. In J. M. Shafritz & C. Hyde (Eds.), *Classics of Organization Theory.* 4th Ed. Orlando, FL: Harcourt Brace & Co.

Sherman, L. (1980). Causes of police behavior: The current state of quantitative research. *Journal of Research in Crime and Delinquency 17,* 69-100.

Skolnick, J. (1966). *Justice without trial: Law enforcement in a democratic society.* New York, NY: John Wiley and Sons.

Skolnick, J. H., & Fyfe, J. J. (1993). *Above the law: Police and the excessive use of force.* New York, NY: The Free Press.

Skolnick, J. H., & McCoy, C. (1984). Police accountability and the media. *American Bar Foundation Research Journal, 3,* 521-557.

Smith, B. Jr. (1960). *Police systems in the United States.* New York, NY: Harper Row.

Smith, D. A. (1984). The organizational aspects of legal control. *Criminology 22,* 19-38.

Smith, D. A., and Klein, J. R. (1983). Police agency characteristics and arrest decisions. In *Evaluating Performance of Criminal Justice Agencies,* ed. G. P. Whitaker and C. D. Phillips. Beverly Hills, CA: Sage.

Swanson, C. R., Territo, L. & Taylor, R. W. (1988). *Police administration: structures, processes, and behavior.* New York, NY: Macmillan Publishing Co.

Tennessee v. Garner, 471 U.S. 1 (1985).

Terry v. Ohio, 392 U.S. 1 (1968).

Toch, H. (1965). *The social psychology of social movements.* Indianapolis, IA: Bobbs-Merrill.

Toch, H., Grant J. D., & Galvin, R. T. (1975). *Agents of change: a study in police reform.* New York, NY: Halstead Press Division.

Vance, J. (1997). *Media relations for the law enforcement executive.* Seminar class presented at the FBI National Academy. Quantico, VA.

Vollmer, A. (1931). The police executive. In *Wickersham Commission Reports,* 14: Report on police, (pp. 17-52). Washington D.C.: U.S. Government Printing Office, 1968.

Walker, S. (1993). *Taming the system: The control of discretion in criminal justice 1950-1990.* New York, NY: Oxford University Press.

Walker, S. (2001). *Police accountability: The role of citizen oversight.* Belmont, CA: Wadsworth/Thompson Learning.

Westly, W. A. (1970). *Violence and the police: A sociological study of law, custom, and morality.* Cambridge, MA: MIT Press.

Wickersham Commission (1931). *Report on police.* Washington, DC: U.S. Government Printing Office.

Wilson, J. Q. (1968). *Varieties of police behavior.* Cambridge, MA: Harvard University Press.

Wilson, J. Q., & Kelling, G. L. (1982). Broken windows: The police and neighborhood safety. *The Atlantic Monthly, March, 1982,* 29-38.

Wilson, O. W., & McLaren, R. C. (1972). *Police administration.* 3rd Ed. New York, NY: McGraw-Hill.

Witkin, G. (1998) Why crime is down: The real story. *U.S. News & World Report, May,* 28-39.

INDEX

A

accountability *4, 5, 6, 13, 14, 18, 24, 35, 40, 41, 42, 48, 59, 61, 69, 71, 72, 73, 84, 85, 106, 126, 127, 129, 136, 150, 152, 153*
ACLU .... See American Civil Liberties Union
ADCS .... See Arrest Discretion Control Scale.
administrative rulemaking..*5 6, 60, 61, 78, 135*
Amadou Diallo *42*
American Bar Foundation *1, 62, 152*
American Civil Liberties Union.................. See ACLU
Attica *21*

B

Beta coefficients..........*114, 115*
bobby..................................*17*
bureaucracy*8, 9, 11, 41, 59, 63, 67, 82, 90, 91, 92, 107, 108, 111, 113, 119, 132, 133, 149, 150*

C

Christopher Commission.*5, 36, 51, 61*
civil rights*5, 14, 24, 50, 51, 70, 83, 138*
Civil Rights Movement *20*
civilian review boards ...*18, 49, 56, 71, 72*
closed system organization...*26*

community policing *13, 14, 18, 69, 70, 71, 72, 73, 85, 107, 123, 126, 128, 129, 148, 150*
contingency theory *2, 26*
crime control ... *8, 9, 36, 53, 70, 90*
cross-classification.. See Police Agencies.

D

deadly force.. *2, 3, 59, 139, 149*
department size ... *9, 11, 90, 91, 111, 114, 136*
dependent variable *8, 89, 93, 95, 114, 115, 116, 118, 130, 137*
Dirty Harry *See* siege mentality

E

employee organizations ..... See unions
environmental constraints *66*

F

FBI Uniform Crime Reports .*2, 59*
fraternal *7, 53, 76, 81, 83*

J

Judicial review *49*

K

Kent State....................*21, 150*

L

legal review ... *79, 87, 124, 126, 143*

legalistic .. *7, 10, 53, 76, 81, 91, 112, 129*

Los Angeles Police Department *20, 22, 50, 56, 149, 152*

M

militaristic *7, 10, 53, 76, 81, 85, 91, 106, 112*

ministerial paradigm *1, 62*

Monell *51, 52, 151*

multicollinearity *116, 118*

O

Open systems theory *26*

order maintenance *8, 23, 42, 53*

organization theory .. *13, 25, 26, 30*

organizational controls *67*

organizational influence .. *8, 11, 75, 76, 77, 82, 86, 89, 92, 93, 106, 109, 121, 123, 124, 131, 132, 139*

organizational structure .. *14, 67*

organizational variables .. *1, 12, 62, 134*

P

Peelian Reform *17*

Police Advisory Board PAB *44*

police brutality *34, 45, 50*

police culture *35, 36, 58, 64, 84, 85, 106, 129*

police discretion *1, 2, 4, 7, 8, 11, 12, 13, 30, 53, 57, 60,*

62, 65, 73, 77, 79, 80, 81, 121, 132, 134, 150, 151

Police Executive Research Forum *36*

Policy Dimension *87, 126*

political system *5, 33*

Process/Procedure Dimension *87*

Professional Police Administration *5*

professional police agencies .. See Service and Legalistic.

professionalism ... *7, 8, 9, 11, 35, 41, 45, 53, 84, 90, 92, 107, 109, 113, 119, 128, 130, 133, 137*

public choice theory *26*

R

Rampart Area Corruption Investigation *5, 61*

regression coefficient . *114, 117*

Rodney King *22, 24, 51, 147*

S

Section 1983 .... *19, 50, 51*

service . *4, 5, 7, 8, 9, 10, 35, 38, 40, 43, 47, 49, 53, 59, 61, 69, 76, 90, 91, 92, 109, 111*

siege mentality *36*

Social control *24*

span of control .... *8, 10, 11, 91, 93, 112, 113, 118, 119, 122, 130, 131, 132, 136, 138.*

strategic planning process *69*

street-level bureaucrats . *59, 62, 65, 66, 67, 68, 136*

street-level discretion .... See decision-making.

structural-legal *27, 30, 32*

supervision *3, 8, 10, 38, 50, 57, 60, 90, 91, 108, 113, 130, 138, 141*
Systems theory *25, 30*

T

Taylor model *3, 60*
Training Dimension *87, 127*

U

unfettered discretion..........*2, 76*
unions................ See employee organizations .
unit of analysis *5, 13, 61, 77, 86, 97, 139*

V

value systems *69*

values 8, 36, 53, 64, 65, 66, 67, 69, 72, 76, 77, 84, 85, 87, 88, 94, 103, 104, 105, 106, 107, 113, 115, 116, 117, 118, 122, 123, 124, 125, 128, 129, 136
Values Dimension........*87, 128*

W

watchman style *7, 53*
Watts Riot *20*
Wickersham Commission*5, 18, 61, 153*

Z

zero-order........................... *108*

Printed in the United States
90994LV00009B/7/A